Decades of American History

CHRONOLOGY OF 20th-CENTURY AMERICA

MELINDA COREY

☑®
Facts On File, Inc.

A Stonesong Press Book
Decades of American History: *Chronology of 20th-Century America*

Copyright © 2006 by Stonesong Press, LLC

Facts On File, Inc.
132 West 31st Street
New York NY 10001

Library of Congress Cataloging-in-Publication Data

Corey, Melinda.
  Chronology of 20th-century America / Melinda Corey.
      p. cm.—(Decades of American history)
  Includes bibliographical references and index.
  ISBN 0-8160-5646-3
  1. United States—History—20th century—Chronology—Juvenile literature.
I. Title. II. Series.
  E741.C585 2005
  973.91'02'02—dc22

                                                    2005013398

Facts On File books are available at special discounts when purchased in bulk quantities
for businesses, associations, institutions, or sales promotions. Please call our Special Sales
Department in New York at (212) 967-8800 or (800) 322-8755.

You can find Facts On File on the World Wide Web at http://www.factsonfile.com

Text design by Laura Smyth, Smythetype
Photo research by Larry Schwartz
Cover design by Pehrsson Design

Printed in the United States of America

VB PKG 10 9 8 7 6 5 4 3 2 1

This book is printed on acid-free paper.

CONTENTS

Chapter 1
1900–1909 • 5

Chapter 2
1910–1919 • 11

Chapter 3
1920–1929 • 21

Chapter 4
1930–1939 • 32

Chapter 5
1940–1949 • 49

Chapter 6
1950–1959 • 62

Chapter 7
1960–1969 • 74

Chapter 8
1970–1979 • 86

Chapter 9
1980–1989 • 99

Chapter 10
1990–1999 • 111

GLOSSARY • 120

FURTHER READING • 122

INDEX • 124

1900–1909

THE FIRST DECADE OF THE 20TH-CENTURY BEGAN IN AMERICA with optimism. President William McKinley championed a United States of 76 million people in 1900, but his term ended in September 1901 when he was killed by anarchist Leon Czolgosz. Vice president and Spanish-American war hero Theodore Roosevelt took over, becoming the youngest president up to that time. Roosevelt brought progressive ideas to his two terms, initiating conservation programs, food and drug legislation, and trust-busting suits to reduce the power of big business. Equally ambitious overseas, he orchestrated the building of the Panama Canal and increased U.S. influence in the Philippines. In 1908, Roosevelt selected William Howard Taft as his successor as president and leader of the Republican Party.

Technology advanced this decade, as did social reform. The Wright brothers made their first historic flight, Henry Ford produced the first Model T automobile, and explorers made it to the North Pole for the first time. New York City began construction its famous underground subway. People around the nation banded together to demand better conditions in many aspects of their lives. African-American leaders formed the National Association for the Advancement of Colored People (NAACP), while muckraking writers exposed the perils of the food industry. The government was forced to listen and passed new food safety laws, as labor unions began to form and make themselves heard.

As President Taft brought the nation into the next decade, technology and social movements continued to advance domestically. Overseas however, unrest was brewing.

1900

- The 1900 census records that the population of the United States is 75,994,575.

- One percent of Americans own 50 percent of U.S. wealth.

- There are 8,000 automobiles in use in the United States.

- The hamburger is introduced at a Connecticut restaurant.

- Notable novels published include *Sister Carrie* by Theodore Dreiser and *The Wonderful Wizard of Oz* by L. Frank Baum.

"The road to the City of Emeralds is paved with yellow brick."

—Lyman Frank Baum, *The Wonderful Wizard of Oz,* 1900

"I am as strong as a bull moose and you can use me to the limit."

—Theodore Roosevelt, 1900

William McKinley was the third president assassinated in office. *(Smithsonian Institute)*

Spanish-American War hero Theodore Roosevelt became president in 1901. *(Library of Congress)*

■ *January 30:* Baseball's American League is formed in Chicago.

■ *September 8:* The deadliest hurricane to date pounds the Texas Gulf Coast, killing 6,000 people. The city of Galveston is nearly destroyed.

■ *November 6:* President McKinley is elected to a second term, defeating Democrat William Jennings Bryan. McKinley's vice president is Theodore Roosevelt.

1901

■ Notable books include the muckraking novel *The Octopus* by Frank Norris and the autobiography *Up From Slavery* by Booker T. Washington.

■ *March 3*: Financier J. P Morgan buys industrialist Andrew Carnegie's steel company, founding the U.S. Steel Corporation.

■ *September 6:* At the Pan-American Exposition in Buffalo, New York, President McKinley is shot by anarchist Leon Czolgosz.

■ *September 14:* President McKinley dies at 2:15 A.M.

■ *September 14:* At age 43, vice-president Theodore Roosevelt becomes the youngest U.S. president to date.

■ *December:* African-American leader Booker T. Washington is invited to the White House.

1902

■ Air conditioning is developed by Willis Carrier.

■ Notable books include the novels *The Wings of the Dove* by Henry James and *The Virginian* by Owen Wister; nonfiction includes *Democracy and Social Action* by reformer Jane Addams and *The Story of My Life* by Helen Keller.

■ *February:* President Roosevelt begins his attack on trusts, applying the Sherman Anti-Trust Act to financier J. P. Morgan's Northern Securities empire of companies.

■ *July:* 150,000 anthracite coal miners strike for shorter hours and higher wages. The strike lasts five months and ends with a 10 percent wage increase and a nine-hour day for workers.

1903

■ Industrialist and inventor Henry Ford founds the Ford Motor Company, in Michigan.

■ Mother Jones leads a crusade of 75,000 textile workers in Philadelphia.

■ Edwin S. Porter premieres *The Great Train Robbery*, the first film made in the United States.

■ Notable novels include *The Call of the Wild* by Jack London; nonfiction includes *The Souls of Black Folk: Essays and Sketches* by W. E. B. Du Bois.

■ *October 1–13:* In the first World Series, the Boston Red Sox/Beaneaters (American League) defeat the Pittsburgh Pirates (National League), five games to three.

■ *December 17:* Ohio bicycle-shop owners Orville and Wilbur Wright test the heavier-than-air airplane in four flights at Kitty Hawk, North Carolina. Orville completes a twelve-second flight of about 120 feet. Wilbur flies for 59 seconds and covers 852 feet.

1904

■ The United States begins construction on the Panama Canal.

■ Notable fiction includes the short story collection *Cabbages and Kings* by O. Henry (William Sydney Porter); nonfiction includes *History of the Standard Oil Company* by Ida Tarbell and *The Shame of the Cities* by Lincoln Steffens.

■ *May 5:* Boston Red Sox pitcher Denton T. "Cy" Young pitches the first perfect game.

■ *October 27:* New York City begins operating the first part of its subway system.

"When you call me that, smile."

—Owen Wister,
The Virginian, 1902

The second flight by the Wright Brothers on December 17, 1903, ran 852 feet and lasted 59 seconds. But the first flight that day ran only 100 feet. They called their plane the Flyer.

"The first requisite of a good citizen in this Republic of ours is that he shall be able and willing to pull his weight."

—Theodore Roosevelt, 1902

TEDDY'S DETRACTORS

Although beloved by much of the public, President Theodore Roosevelt had many critics. Some were politicians who opposed Roosevelt's progressive policies. Conservative politicians believed that Roosevelt's views against big business caused the financial panic of 1907. They and other like-minded senators held such dislike for the so-called bully pulpit president that upon hearing that he would end his term in 1908 with an African safari, they supposedly toasted him by wishing "Health to the lions!"

Outside politics, some of the most vociferous Roosevelt critics were writers. Mark Twain thought Roosevelt was an unforgivable grandstander who was "clearly insane." A longtime antiimperialist, Twain disagreed strongly with Roosevelt's international policies. American expatriate and literary master Henry James also decried Roosevelt's imperialist ways, calling him "a dangerous and ominous jingo [nationalist]." James also thought Roosevelt talked too much. After meeting him in 1904, James called Roosevelt "the mere monstrous embodiment of unprecedented resounding Noise."

This political cartoon from 1904 pokes fun at Roosevelt's foreign policy of "Speak softly and carry a big stick." *(Library of Congress)*

"I believe the power to make money is a gift from God."

—John D. (Davison) Rockefeller, in an interview, 1905

"I aimed at the public's heart, and by accident I hit it in the stomach."

—Upton Sinclair, on his novel *The Jungle*, 1906

▪ *November 8:* President Roosevelt is reelected. Charles W. Fairbanks is vice president. Roosevelt defeats, among others, Democrat Alton B. Parker and Socialist Eugene V. Debs.

1905

▪ There are 77,988 automobiles registered in the United States.

▪ Notable novels include *The House of Mirth* by Edith Wharton and *The Clansman* by Thomas Dixon Jr.

▪ *July 7:* The international labor group, Industrial Workers of the World (IWW), or Wobblies, is formed in Chicago.

1906

▪ The first national monument is named: Devil's Tower in Wyoming.

- W. E. B. Du Bois founds the Niagara Movement, to promote the civil rights of African Americans.

- President Roosevelt becomes the first American to win a Nobel Prize when he receives the Peace Prize for brokering an end to the Russo-Japanese War.

- Notable literature includes *The Jungle* by Upton Sinclair, *The Four Million,* by O. Henry, and *The Spirit of the Border,* by Zane Grey.

- *March 17:* In a speech, President Roosevelt uses the term *muckraker* to describe investigative writers such as Upton Sinclair and Ida Tarbell, who draw attention to elements of society that need reform.

- *April 7:* The first transatlantic radio transmission is made, from New York to Ireland.

- *April 18:* A massive earthquake destroys much of San Francisco and kills more than 700 people. Most of the property damage is caused by fires that follow the quake.

1907

- More than 1 million immigrants pass through New York's Ellis Island

- "Mr. Mutt," the first daily comic strip, appears in the *San Francisco Chronicle*. It will later be named "Mutt and Jeff."

- Outbreaks of typhoid fever are traced to a cook in New York City named Mary Mallon, known as Typhoid Mary.

- Notable books include *Pragmatism* by psychologist and philosopher William James.

- *May:* Mother's Day is celebrated for the first time, in West Virginia.

- *October:* The Chicago Cubs (NL) win the World Series against the Detroit Tigers (AL).

- *November 16*: Oklahoma becomes the 46th state.

The San Francisco earthquake lasted only seconds on April 18, 1906, but the fires it created lasted three days. When they subsided, 500 people were dead and 225,000 had lost their homes.

Roosevelt's promise of a "square deal" for every American made him very popular with the people. *(Library of Congress)*

"Take me out to the ball game,
Take me out with the crowd."

—Jack Norworth, *Take Me Out to the Ball Game,* 1908

William Howard Taft was chosen by Theodore Roosevelt to carry on the square deal. *(Library of Congress)*

IN THE MUCK

President Roosevelt's term *muckraking* demonstrated his opinion of the first investigative journalists. Journalist Upton Sinclair exposed the horrors of the meat-packing industry in *The Jungle.* It described wage slavery and horrific conditions that were extremely unsafe and unsanitary. The public outcry following the publication of the novel led to historic federal legislation and fueled other muckraking exposés.

1908

- The U.S. Bureau of Investigation is founded. It will develop into the Federal Bureau of Investigation (FBI).

- The General Motors Company is founded.

- The vacuum cleaner is developed.

- Notable books published include *The Trail of the Lonesome Pines* by John Fox Jr. and *The Circular Staircase* by Mary Roberts Rinehart.

- *October 1:* Henry Ford introduces the Model T.

- *November 3:* Republican William Howard Taft is elected president. James Sherman is vice president.

- *December 26:* American fighter Jack Johnson defeats Canadian Tommy Burns for the world heavyweight boxing title. Johnson is the first fighter of African descent to win the title.

1909

- The Homestead Act of 1909 spurs further settlement in the West.

- W. E. B. Du Bois, Oswald Garrison Villard, and others form the National Association for the Advancement of Colored People (NAACP).

- Notable books include the story collection *Three Lives* by Gertrude Stein and novel *Martin Eden* by Jack London.

- *April 6:* Explorer Robert Edwin Peary and his team are the first in history to reach the North Pole.

- *October 8–16:* The Pittsburgh Pirates (NL) defeat the Detroit Tigers (AL) in the World Series.

CHAPTER 2

1910–1919

D ISSATISFIED WITH THE COUNTRY'S LEADERSHIP, FORMER president Theodore Roosevelt returned to politics in 1912 with the Bull Moose Party. His candidacy in that race split the Republican vote, and the nation elected Democrat Woodrow Wilson.

The country continued to grow, adding Arizona and New Mexico as states. Henry Ford began using the assembly line to manufacture his cars, dropping the selling price dramatically. Now automobile ownership was accessible to many more "regular" Americans. Labor unions continued to grow and strengthen. Among other improvements, the eight-hour workday was established. Prohibition was also established, making the sale and consumption of alcohol illegal. Although many Americans supported the amendment, many others found ways around it, visiting illegal speakeasies and arranging deals with bootleggers.

The unrest Europe erupted into war in 1914, and President Wilson resisted U.S. involvement. But German attacks on U.S. ships eventually led Wilson to declare war. By mid-1918, 1 million U.S. troops were winning battles overseas, and in November 1918, Germany agreed to an armistice, ending the conflict. In summer 1919, the Treaty of Versailles was signed, and President Wilson tried to build world peace through his efforts to make the United States join the League of Nations. But in November of that year, the U.S. Senate rejected the treaty. The United States was not concerned with international peacemaking; it was interested in returning to normalcy.

1910

- The 1910 census reading is 91,972,266 U.S. residents.

- The so-called Great Migration of blacks from the rural South to northern cities begins.

- The rate of U.S. illiteracy reaches a new low: 7.7 percent.

- There are 500,000 automobiles in use in the United States

- Baseball attendance reaches 7 million.

- Notable books include the novel *The Rosary* by Florence Barclay and the poetry collection *The Town Down the River* by Edward Arlington Robinson.

"HELLO OPERATOR"

Placing calls for the more than 1 million telephones in the early 20th century was a big job, done not by a computer but by a person, the central exchange operator, who physically connected callers by plugging wires into a board. The very first telephone exchange operators were teenage boys, who had been telegraph operators and delivery boys. But they tended to be rude and mischievous; many discipline problems occurred, customers complained, and they were replaced. In the early 20th century, job discrimination was openly practiced, and so men, as well as blacks and other minorities were excluded from operator jobs.

That operator was almost always a young woman chosen for her quick thinking and sweet voice. New York Telephone Company called their operators "The Voice with a Smile."

By 1910, there were 7 million telephones in the United States. *(AT&T)*

■ *February 6:* The Boy Scouts of America is founded.

■ *October 17–23:* The Philadelphia Athletics (AL) win the World Series against the Chicago Cubs NL).

1911

■ The Chevrolet Motor Company is founded by W. C. Durant.

■ Notable books include *Ethan Frome* by Edith Wharton; nonfiction includes *The Devil's Dictionary* by Ambrose Bierce and *The Mind of Primitive Man,* by anthropologist Franz Boas.

■ *March 25:* The Triangle Shirtwaist Company in New York catches fire killing 146, many of whom jump to their death to escape the fire. Exit doors had been locked to prevent workers from leaving their work area.

■ *May 15:* U.S. Supreme Court calls for the Standard Oil trust to be dissolved.

■ *October 14–26:* The Philadelphia Athletics (AL) defeats the New York Giants (NL) in the World Series.

1912

■ The F. W. Woolworth Company is founded. Its stores become a feature of small-town America.

Young female textile workers worked long hours for low wages often living in industrial housing far from home. *(Library of Congress)*

- Notable novels include *The Financier* by Theodore Dreiser and *Confessions of an Ex-Colored Man* by James Weldon Johnson.

- *January 6:* New Mexico becomes the 47th state.

- *January 12:* The Industrial Workers of the World (IWW) lead a textile strike in Lawrence, Massachusetts. The six-week strike will result in higher wages and reduced hours for workers, and increased prestige for the IWW.

- *February 14:* Arizona becomes the 48th state.

- *April 14:* On its maiden voyage, British ocean liner *Titanic* hits an iceberg and sinks. About 1,500 people died at sea because the ship lacked sufficient lifeboats.

- *May 5–July 22:* James Francis (Jim) Thorpe, an American Indian, wins the decathlon and pentathlon at the Stockholm Olympics.

- *June 19:* Congress passes a law granting federal workers an eight-hour workday.

- *October 8–16:* The Boston Red Sox (AL) defeat the New York Giants (NL) in the World Series.

Because Jim Thorpe accepted payment for appearing in semiprofessional games, he lost his Olympic medals in 1913. Today, professional athletes are permitted to compete in the Olympics. (*AP/Wide World*)

One of the *Titanic*'s lifeboats carries survivors to safety the following morning. (*Library of Congress*)

Wilson served as president of Princeton University from 1902–1910. In 1912, he was elected president of the United States. *(Princeton University Library)*

By the end of World War I, about 4.8 million Americans had served in the armed forces. Nearly two-thirds of the funds to pay for them and their war effort came from Liberty Bond drives that raised money by selling bonds to the public.

■ *October 14:* Theodore Roosevelt is wounded in an assassination attempt.

■ *November 5:* Democrat Woodrow Wilson is elected president. He defeats Republican William Howard Taft and Progressive (Bull Moose) Theodore Roosevelt.

1913

■ The Woolworth Building is completed in New York City. At 792 feet, it is the tallest building in the world to date.

■ Grand Central Terminal opens in New York City.

■ The Olympic Committee takes away the medals Jim Thorpe won in 1912 because of questions about his amateur status after it is revealed that Thorpe played semiprofessional football in 1909.

■ Notable movies include Cecil B. DeMille's *The Straw Man*, a pioneering example of a feature (full-length) film.

■ Notable literary works include Willa Cather's novel *O Pioneers!*, the children's novel *Pollyanna* by Eleanor Hodgman Porter; poems include the collection *General William Booth Enters Heaven* by Vachel Lindsay and Joyce Kilmer's poem "Trees."

■ *February 17:* Postimpressionist and cubist art is introduced to the American public at the International Exhibition of Modern Art, also known as the Armory Show, in New York City.

■ *February 25:* Income tax is introduced with the passage of the Sixteenth Amendment to the Constitution.

■ *Summer:* The Ford Motor Company begins to use the assembly line to build the Model T.

■ *October 7–11:* The Philadelphia Athletics (AL) defeat the New York Giants (NL) in the World Series.

■ *December 23:* The Federal Reserve System is created, establishing a central banking system meant to promote U.S. economic stability.

LIVES OF THE BARONS

The powerful businessmen who controlled oil, steel, and financial corporations in the early 20th-century were often called barons. Some of them were considered more powerful than the president. Most of them started with nothing or grew up in poverty. Their so-called rags to riches stories became part of American mythology.

Andrew Carnegie worked in a Pittsburgh factory before he built a local steel mill into a empire that he sold to financier John Pierpont Morgan for $480 million in 1900. That much money was commonplace to J. P. Morgan, born into one of America's largest banking dynasties. The world's richest man at the time, however, John D. Rockefeller, who also started poor. Like Carnegie, he rose from a lowly job as an office clerk in Cleveland to build an oil refinery and form the Standard Oil Company, worth $1 billion in 1910.

Although these barons enjoyed power, none tried to expand their reach to politics. Instead, they served the public indirectly: Carnegie founded public libraries, Morgan funded museums and hospitals, and many Rockefeller descendants became reform-minded politicians.

1914

- President Wilson signs the Clayton Antitrust Act, which grants unions the right to strike, boycott, and picket.

- Nurse and women's advocate Margaret Sanger coins the term *birth control* and publishes the flyer *Family Limitation*.

- Notable novels include *Tarzan of the Apes* by Edgar Rice Burroughs and *Penrod* by Booth Tarkington; poetry includes the collection *North of Boston* by Robert Frost.

- *July 28:* Archduke Franz Ferdinand and wife are assassinated in Sarajevo. Austria declares war on Serbia. Other countries issue declarations of war within days.

- *August 15:* The U.S.-built Panama Canal opens. The cost is $366,650,000.

- *October 9–13:* The Boston Braves (NL) defeat the Philadelphia Athletics (AL) in the World Series.

1915

- The Ku Klux Klan reorganizes. It is a secretive organization that promotes the belief that African Americans and other non-whites and Catholics and other non-Protestants are inferior to white Protestants.

"Don't waste any time mourning— organize!"

—Joe (Joseph Hillstrom) Hill, an American labor activist, in a letter to William Haywood, day before Hill's execution, 1915

BORN IN THE U.S.A.

In the 20th century, even the very beginning of life changed radically. For centuries, most women gave birth at home. In the early 1900s, professionalized and medicated childbirth started to become popular. Doctors and drugs replaced midwives and Bibles.

In the 19th century, most women prepared days before the expected birth by entering the lying-in phase, during which she waited in a quiet room with female family, friends, and midwife. Ministers taught that childbirth pain was sanctioned by the Bible. Men were admitted to the room only after childbirth had taken place.

The introduction of anesthesia, or pain relief, in the mid-19th century changed childbirth attitudes. Women embraced findings in books such as Marguerite Tracy's *Painless Childbirth* (1915), which championed hospital deliveries and anesthesia. By the late 1910s, a study of two states showed that midwife delivery (for white women) had dropped to 16 percent. Poor mothers went to the hospital charity wards, while middle- and upper-class women increasingly gave birth in private hospitals, under anesthesia and attended by physicians.

The Panama Canal was an engineering marvel because of its huge locks—dams with gates that permitted water levels to be raised and lowered as ships passed through.
(Library of Congress)

- The victrola, or phonograph, is introduced by the Victor Talking Machine Company.

- Notable movies include D. W. Griffith's *The Birth of a Nation*. It arouses protest for its positive presentation of the Ku Klux Klan.

- Notable poetry includes Edgar Lee Masters's collection *Spoon River Anthology* and Robert Frost's poem "The Road Not Taken"; novels include *The Song of the Lark* by Willa Cather.

- *January 25:* The first transcontinental telephone call is made, from San Francisco.

- *May 7:* The British ocean liner *Lusitania* is sunk by a German submarine, killing 1,198 passengers, 128 of whom are American. The incident ignites American support for entering the war in Europe.

- *October 8–13:* The Boston Red Sox (AL) defeat the Philadelphia Phillies (NL) in the World Series.

1916

- Twenty-four states have prohibition laws.

- There are about 3,500,000 cars in the United States.

- Notable films include D. W. Griffith's *Intolerance*.

Mexican revolutionary Pancho Villa (on horse, center) raided American border towns in 1916. Wilson told General Pershing "Capture Villa, dead or alive." *(Library of Congress)*

■ Notable fiction includes the short story collection *The Rising Tide* by James Branch Cabell and novel *Seventeen* by Booth Tarkington; nonfiction includes John Dewey's *Democracy and Education.*

■ *March 9:* Mexican Francisco Pancho Villa and troops make raids into New Mexico, killing 17 Americans.

■ *June 1:* Louis Brandeis becomes the first Jewish person to become a justice of the Supreme Court.

■ *August 25:* The National Park Service is established.

■ *October 7–12:* The Boston Red Sox (AL) defeat the Brooklyn Dodgers (NL) in the World Series.

■ *October 16:* Margaret Sanger opens the first birth control clinic, in Brooklyn, New York.

■ *November 7:* Woodrow Wilson defeats Republican Charles Evans Hughes and is reelected president. Thomas R. Marshall is reelected vice president.

1917

■ The Espionage Act is passed, prohibiting protesters from speaking or demonstrating against the war.

> *"The world must be made safe for democracy."*
>
> —Woodrow Wilson, address to Congress, asking for declaration of war, 1917

Henry Ford's Model T revolutionized the automobile industry, selling more than 15 million between 1908 and 1926. The mass-produced car revolutionized American life as well, changing where people lived and how they lived forever. *(Ford Motor Company)*

■ Congress mandates literacy tests for immigrants, which lowers the number of immigrants entering the United States.

■ Notable novels include *Susan Lenox: Her Fall and Rise* by David Graham Phillips; poetry includes T. S. Eliot's poem "The Love Song of J. Alfred Prufrock" and Edna St. Vincent Millay's collection *Renascence.*

■ *February 3:* German U-boats sink the USS *Housatonic.* Three more boats will be sunk on March 16.

■ *February 24:* German foreign minister Arthur Zimmermann proposes that Germany and Mexico form an alliance if the United States enters war.

■ *March 1:* The Zimmermann letter is made public, and many Americans are outraged.

■ *March 2:* Puerto Rico becomes a U.S. territory.

■ *April 6:* The United States enters World War I as a member of the Allied Forces.

■ *October 6–15:* The Chicago White Sox (AL) defeat the New York Giants (NL) in the World Series.

"The Yanks are coming..../And we won't come back till it's over over there."

—George M. Cohan,
Over There, 1917

- *November 3:* The United States enters its first battle of the war, around the Rhine-Marne Canal, France.

1918

- More than 2 million U.S. soldiers fight in France.

- U.S. war deaths total more than 53,000 from battle and more than 63,000 from other causes.

- Socialist leader Eugene V. Debs is sentenced to ten years in prison for opposition to World War I.

- Pandemic of Spanish influenza results in 500,000 U.S. deaths.

- Notable literature includes *The Autobiography of Henry Adams,* released widely after private publication in 1907.

- *January 8:* President Wilson presents the international peace proposal, the Fourteen Points.

- *March 21–April 6:* German forces are defeated by the Allies in the Somme offensive.

- *May 16:* The Sedition Act is passed, prohibiting antiwar language in speech or print.

- *September 5–11:* The Boston Red Sox defeat the Chicago Cubs (NL) in the World Series.

- *November 11:* Germany agrees to an armistice, which ends the fighting in World War I. The war officially ends on the eleventh hour of the eleventh day of the eleventh month of the year.

1919

- Attorney General A. Mitchell Palmer stages raids on radical political groups in the United States in an attempt to prevent communism from gaining ground. This anticommunist reaction is known as a Red Scare, because the color red is associated with communism.

The stalemate of trench warfare led to extremely high fatalities in World War I. These German soldiers wear masks to protect themselves from gas attacks. *(National Archives)*

PATRIOTIC FOOD

During World War I, anti-German sentiment ran high and took many forms. Some state and local governments and restaurants renamed popular German foods. Sauerkraut was soon called liberty cabbage, and hamburgers (named for the German city of Hamburg) were known as Salisbury steak. In some towns, sales of pretzels, popularized by German immigrants, were prohibited.

"How You Gonna Keep 'Em Down on the Farm After They've Seen Paree?"

—Sam M. Lewis & Joe Young, title and refrain of 1919 song talking about soldiers who had seen Paris for the first time

A**utobat, motorfly, and viamote were early suggestions for what eventually was called the automobile. By 1919, the automobile, or car, was a fixture on U.S. city and town streets.**

WHAT AMERICANS ATE

The early 20th-century American dinner table was quite different from the dinner table of a century later. Without fast shipping and advanced technology, food had to come from local farms and home kitchens. In 1900, the well-to-do ate multicourse meals prepared by cooks and servants. A dinner would include soup, at least one meat, vegetables, and homemade breads and pastries. Less prosperous families bought less expensive cuts of meat; ate fresh vegetables from their garden or vegetables that women and servants had put up, or preserved in glass jars months earlier; and ate homemade bread. Prepared foods such as canned vegetables were exotic novelties. Poorer families often centered meals around foods made from cheap starches, such as flour or potatoes. By 1919, frozen and canned foods were more widely used, so some seasonal vegetables like asparagus could be canned and were available year-round. Fresh tropical produce was still rare for many families, so that an orange was a Christmas treat.

- Dockworkers and steelworkers hold major strikes.

- Notable literary works include Sherwood Anderson's story collection *Winesburg, Ohio* and H. L. Mencken's study, *The American Language.*

- *January 29:* The Eighteenth Amendment to the Constitution, or Prohibition, is ratified. It prohibits the manufacture, sale, or transportation of alcoholic beverages.

- *February 14:* The first draft of the document creating the League of Nations is presented in France by President Wilson.

- *June 11:* Sir Barton wins the Kentucky Derby (at Churchill Downs, Kentucky), the Preakness Stakes (in Baltimore, Maryland), and the Belmont Stakes (in New York) to become the first horse to win the Triple Crown of horse racing.

- *June 28:* The Treaty of Versailles between Germany and the Allied Forces is signed.

- *September 26:* President Wilson suffers a serious stroke.

- *October 1–9:* The Cincinnati Reds (NL) defeat the Chicago White Sox (AL) in the World Series.

CHAPTER 3

1920–1929

T HE UNITED STATES RESUMED LIFE AFTER THE GREAT WAR, AS World War I was called, with soberness and self-confidence. Soldiers who had fought in the war were changed by the experience, broadened in their view of world affairs or worn out by the experience of seeing thousands of lives lost. For most civilians, though, the end of the war meant returning to normal and trying to make up for wartime sacrifices. To do so, they elected business-oriented Republican presidents Warren Harding, Calvin Coolidge, and Herbert Hoover. The internationalism of President Woodrow Wilson (who died in 1921) withered as the United States decided not to enter the League of Nations. Despite political isolation, the country grew more culturally sophisticated, thanks to technology and industrialization. New technologies brought jobs into cities, and Ford's assembly-line cars and multiple forms of mass transportation brought workers to jobs. Transportation also took Americans to pleasure centers such as Atlantic City and Coney Island and to baseball games, which continued to expand in popularity. Americans also found ways to break the laws of Prohibition and get the liquor they wanted. Speculating in the stock market attracted many Americans, and their investments sent the stock market to historic heights. Then on October 29, 1929, the market lost much of its value, a process that continued for weeks. In total, nearly $30 billion of stock value was lost. The Great Depression had begun.

1920

- According to the 1920 census, the population of United States is 106,021,537.

- Urban residents outnumber rural residents. According to the 1920 census, 54 million are urban dwellers, 51 million are rural dwellers. For the first time in census history, rural dwellers make up less than 50 percent of the population.

- The median age of Americans is 25.3.

- The average life expectancy, according to the Bureau of Public Health, is 54.09 years.

- The U.S. illiteracy rate is 6 percent, the lowest to date.

"This law will be obeyed in cities, large and small, and in villages, and where it is not obeyed it will be enforced."

—John F. Kramer, Prohibition commissioner, on the strong enforcement of the Volstead Act banning liquor production and consumption, 1920

Republican presidential candidate Senator Warren Harding conducted a winning campaign in 1920 by staying in his hometown in Ohio. There he was a regular guy who pitched horseshoes, played poker, and lived the life of normalcy that he promised to bring to the voters.

President Warren G. Harding addresses the U.S. House of Representatives. *(Library of Congress)*

■ Notable novels published include *Main Street* by Sinclair Lewis, *This Side of Paradise* by F. Scott Fitzgerald, and *The Age of Innocence* by Edith Wharton.

■ *April 15:* In South Braintree, Massachusetts, paymaster Frank Parmenter and factory guard Alexander Bernardelli are shot and killed. The men accused are Sacco and Vanzetti, and the case becomes world famous.

■ *April 20–September 12:* The Olympics is held in Antwerp, Belgium. The United States wins nine gold medals.

■ *July 9–16:* The United States wins the Davis Cup international tennis competition for the first time.

■ *September 7–11:* The first transcontinental airmail plane carries cargo from New York to California.

■ *September 28:* Eight members of the Chicago White Sox baseball team (AL) are indicted on bribery charges, accused of taking bribes to lose the World Series to the Cincinnati Reds. The team is called the Black Sox.

■ *October 5–12:* The Cleveland Indians (AL) defeat the Brooklyn Dodgers (NL) to win the World Series.

■ *November 2:* Republican candidate Warren G. Harding is elected president. His vice president is Calvin Coolidge.

■ *November 2:* Pittsburgh radio station KDKA broadcasts the results of the presidential election, becoming the first radio station to transmit information to the general public.

■ *November 20:* President Woodrow Wilson is awarded the Nobel Peace Prize.

1921

■ A depression begins in United States during midyear.

■ The Volstead Act generates strong business outside the law for bootleggers, home liquor makers, and liquor importers.

- The American Federation of Labor has about 4,000,000 members.

- Notable novels include *The Sheik* by Edith W. Hull, *Alice Adams* by Booth Tarkington, and *Three Soldiers* by John Dos Passos.

- *January 13:* The Census Bureau reports that 51 percent of Americans inhabit towns of more than 2,500.

- *May 19:* Congress passes a quota-based immigration act, the first such law to limit U.S. immigration.

- *June 25:* Samuel Gompers becomes president of the American Federation of Labor (AFL).

- *August:* The Ku Klux Klan is revived in the South; it is responsible for both property damage and personal attacks in the forms of lynching, tarring, and whipping. Targets are African Americans and non-Protestant whites.

- *August 2:* The Chicago White Sox players involved in the Black Sox scandal of 1921 are banned from the game by Judge Kenesaw Mountain Landis.

- *August 25:* The United States and Germany sign a peace treaty in Berlin.

- *September 8:* The first Miss America pageant is held in Atlantic City, New Jersey. It is won by Margaret Gorman, the contestant from Washington, D.C.

- *October 5–13:* The New York Giants (NL) defeat the New York Yankees (AL) in the World Series. It is broadcast on the radio for the first time.

- *November 5:* Armistice Day is proclaimed a national holiday to be held on November 11 yearly.

- *November 11:* The remains of an unknown soldier of World War I are buried at Arlington National Cemetery. The grave symbolizes the unidentified dead.

Eliot Ness became a well-known opponent of gangsters such as Al Capone. *(Corbis)*

Bootlegger and career criminal Al Capone maintained a respectable office in Chicago, Illinois, as a front for his illegal activities. His business cards read, "ALPHONSE CAPONE/Second Hand Furniture Dealer/2220 South Wabash Avenue."

"April is the cruellest month"

—T. S. (Thomas Stearns) Eliot,
The Waste Land, 1922

During the 1920s Red Scare, patriotic associations ferreted out communist sympathizers. The Allied Defense Society cited entertainers Charlie Chaplin and Will Rogers as being mentioned in communist files, and the Better America Foundation called education reformer John Dewey "dangerous to young people."

1922

- The Jazz Age, the musical period representing the flowering of jazz music across the country, is in full swing.

- Notable novels include *One of Ours* by Willa Cather, *The Enormous Room* by e. e. cummings, *The Beautiful and Damned* by F. Scott Fitzgerald, and *Babbitt* by Sinclair Lewis; notable poetry includes *The Waste Land* by T. S. Eliot.

- *February 27:* The Supreme Court declares the Nineteenth Amendment to the Constitution constitutional. The amendment allows for women's suffrage.

- *April 15:* In a Senate investigation, Secretary of the Interior Albert B. Fall is asked why the Teapot Dome oil lands meant for the U.S. Navy were leased to the Mammoth Oil Company.

- *May 30:* The Lincoln Memorial is dedicated in Washington, D.C.

- *June 14:* President Warren G. Harding is the first president to be heard on the radio when he dedicates Baltimore's Francis Scott Key memorial. (Key authored "The Star Spangled Banner," the national anthem.)

- *August 28:* The first radio commercial is broadcast, on WEAF in New York City.

- *October 3:* The first woman U.S. senator, Mrs. W. H. Felton, of Georgia, is appointed by Georgia governor Thomas Hardwick.

- *October 4–8:* The New York Giants (NL) defeat the New York Yankees (AL) in the World Series.

1923

- About 15,000 cars are owned for passenger use in the United States.

- Cellophane, or cellulose film, is produced for the first time in the United States, by the DuPont Corporation.

- The Broadway musical *Running Wild* helps make the Charleston a dance sensation.

- Notable novels include *A Lost Lady* by Willa Cather and *Streets of Night* by John Dos Passos; *New Hampshire: A Poem With Notes and Grace Notes* by Robert Frost, *Collected Poems* by Vachel Lindsay, *Harmonium* by Wallace Stevens, and *Cane* by Jean Toomer.

- *January:* Reporters use the words *fundamentalist* and *modernist* to describe the two sides of the debate on the theory of evolution. The terms become part of public debate.

- *July 15:* Robert T. "Bobby" Jones, an amateur, wins the U.S. Open golf tournament.

- *August 2:* President Warren G. Harding dies at age 58. On a tour to the western United States, he contracted ptomaine poisoning and pneumonia. Recovering in San Francisco, he suffered an embolism and died.

- *August 3:* at 2:43 A.M. Vice President Calvin Coolidge is sworn in as president.

- *September 15:* Oklahoma is placed under martial law following terrorist activities by the Ku Klux Klan.

- *October 10–15:* The New York Yankees (AL) defeat the New York Giants (NL) in the World Series, four games to two.

1924

- Automobiles made by Ford reach their lowest price: $290.

- Notable novels published include *Billy Budd, Foretopman* by Herman Melville and *The Marble Faun* by William Faulkner; poetry collections include *Tamar and Other Poems* by Robinson Jeffers; nonfiction works include the *Autobiography of Mark Twain* and *How to Write Short Stories* by Ring Lardner.

- *January 1:* There are about 2,500,000 radios in the United States.

Wildly popular actor Rudolph Valentino is depicted on the cover of *Motion Picture* magazine with his second wife, Natacha Rambova. Valentino married her in 1923, but when it was discovered that his divorce from his first wife was not official, he was jailed as a bigamist and fined $10,000. *(Private Collection)*

Warren Harding died unexpectedly, of illness, in California. *(Library of Congress)*

TUNING IN
Between 1922 and 1929, radio sales boomed from $60,000,000 to $842,548,000. Early programming was both practical and commercially oriented. Some stations ran nationality hours in languages common to the region. Advertisers such as battery maker Eveready and grocery chain A & P bought entire programs, which they named for the product. Popular radio singers included Rudy Vallee.

The trial of John Scopes for teaching evolution in Tennessee was symbolic of the divide separating big-city sophistication and small-town conservatism during the 1920s.
(AP/Wide World)

■ *January 25–February 4:* The first Winter Olympics is held in Chamonix, France. The United States places fourth.

■ *June 2:* An amendment to the Constitution protecting children from dangerous child labor practices is introduced.

■ *June 12:* Republicans Calvin Coolidge and running mate Charles Dawes are nominated for reelection at the Republican National Convention.

■ *June 30:* A federal grand jury indicts former Secretary of the Interior Albert Fall and others in the Teapot Dome bribery scandal. Fall, along with Mammoth Oil Company president Harry Sinclair, president of Pan-American Oil and Transport Company Edward L. Doheny, and Edward L. Doheny Jr., are charged with bribery and plans to defraud the government.

■ *July 9:* John W. Davis and running mate Charles Bryan are nominated for president and vice president at the Democratic National Convention.

■ *October 4–10:* The Washington Senators (AL) defeat the New York Giants (NL) in the World Series.

■ *November 4:* Republican president Calvin Coolidge is reelected president of the United States. Charles Dawes is elected vice president.

1925

■ Two magazines aimed at capturing the faster pace of the new century begin publication: the weekly newsmagazine *Time* and the arts and culture weekly *The New Yorker*.

■ Notable novels published include *An American Tragedy* by Theodore Dreiser, *Manhattan Transfer* by John Dos Passos, *The Great Gatsby* by F. Scott Fitzgerald, and *Arrowsmith* by Sinclair Lewis.

■ *July 10–21:* The Scopes trial is held in Dayton, Tennessee. John Scopes is charged with breaking state law by teaching the theory of evolution. He is defended by Clarence Darrow and Dudley Field Malone, while former presidential candidate William Jennings Bryan is one of the prosecutors. Scopes is found guilty and fined $100.

■ *July 26:* Presumably from the stress of the Scopes trial, William Jennings Bryan dies.

■ *August 8:* Forty thousand members of the Ku Klux Klan march in support of their beliefs.

■ *October:* A boom in real estate and land development hits its peak in Florida, as railroads and drainage projects make the state more appealing and easy to reach.

■ *October 7–15:* The Pittsburgh Pirates (NL) defeat the Washington Senators (AL) in the World Series.

1926

■ Industrialist Henry Ford announces the concept of the 40-hour workweek as a means to check unemployment and curb overproduction.

■ Ferdinand "Jelly Roll" Morton begins to make jazz recordings with his band, the Red Hot Peppers.

■ Notable novels include *Soldiers' Pay* by William Faulkner, *The Sun Also Rises* by Ernest Hemingway, and *Topper* by Thorne Smith; poetry includes *The Weary Blues* by Langston Hughes.

■ *March 7:* The first successful transatlantic telephone conversation is made, between New York and London.

■ *May 9:* Rear Admiral Richard Byrd and Floyd Bennett make the first successful flight over the North Pole.

■ *May 10:* U.S. Marines enter Nicaragua to intervene in an uprising by General Augusto Sandino against Emiliano Chamorro, who had taken power in 1925.

■ *July 10:* Robert "Bobby" Jones wins the U.S. Open golf tournament.

> "—Question: If you find so much that is unworthy of reverence in the United States, then why do you live here? —Answer: Why do men go to zoos?"
>
> —H. L. Mencken, *Prejudices, Fifth Series,* 1925

Suburban locales across America gained popularity and population in the 1920s. During the decade, the borough of Queens, New York, doubled in population to more than 1 million. Subdivisions in the Detroit metropolitan area were in such demand that one-room-sized lots were snapped up.

The Ku Klux Klan, led in 1926 by "imperial wizard" H. W. Evans, attracted many new members during the 1920s. *(Library of Congress)*

- *August 6:* American Gertrude Ederle, age 19, is the first woman to swim the English Channel. Her time is 14 hours, 31 minutes.

- *October 2–10*: The St. Louis Cardinals (NL) defeat the New York Yankees in the World Series.

- *November 2:* In Congressional elections, Democrats gain seats, but are still in the minority.

1927

- The monument known as Mount Rushmore is dedicated in South Dakota. Carved into a stone mountainside by Gutzon Borglum, it depicts four U.S. presidents: George Washington, Thomas Jefferson, Abraham Lincoln, and Teddy Roosevelt.

- The 15-millionth Model T Ford is produced.

- George Herman "Babe" Ruth hits a record 60 home runs for the New York Yankees.

- Notable novels include *Elmer Gantry* by Sinclair Lewis, *Oil!* by Upton Sinclair, *The Bridge of San Luis Rey* by Thornton Wilder, and *Death Comes for the Archbishop* by Willa Cather; poetry includes *archy and mehitabel* by Don Marquis.

Quiet, reserved Calvin Coolidge served two terms in the 1920s. *(Library of Congress)*

Charles Lindbergh was greeted with a ticker-tape parade when he returned to New York City after making the first nonstop solo flight across the Atlantic in 1927. *(Library of Congress)*

- *January 7:* Commercial transatlantic telephone service begins, between New York and London.

- *April 7:* Television is demonstrated successfully for the first time, in New York.

- *May 20:* Aviator Charles Lindbergh, 25, departs Roosevelt Field, Long Island, in a monoplane to become the first person to fly solo across the Atlantic Ocean.

- *May 21:* Charles Lindbergh arrives at Orly, France. He is greeted by a crowd of nearly 100,000.

- *July 29:* The iron lung respirator is installed for the first time, at New York's Bellevue Hospital. It allows patients with severe disabilities and paralysis to breathe.

- *August 2:* President Calvin Coolidge declines to run for reelection.

- *August 23:* Nicola Sacco and Bartolomeo Vanzetti are executed in Massachusetts for the 1920 murder of a factory guard. Many groups protest the killing.

- *October 5–8:* The New York Yankees (AL) defeat the Pittsburgh Pirates (NL) in the World Series.

One of America's greatest novelists and short story writers, William Faulkner, published his first novels in the 1920s. *(Private Collection)*

"You ain't heard nothin' yet, folks."

—Al Jolson,
The Jazz Singer, 1927

Edna St. Vincent Millay was a leading poet in the Greenwich Village, New York, set during the 1920s. *(Private Collection)*

- *October 6: The Jazz Singer,* starring Al Jolson, is released. The first film to use sound on film, it is an immediate hit.

- *November 13:* The Holland Tunnel opens, linking New York and New Jersey. It is the first underwater tunnel for motor vehicles.

1928

- Notable novels include *Scarlet Sister Mary* by Julia Peterkin and *The Man Who Knew Coolidge* by Sinclair Lewis; poetry includes *John Brown's Body* by Stephen Vincent Benét, *West-Running Brook* by Robert Frost, *Buck in the Snow* by Edna St. Vincent Millay, and *Good Morning, America* by Carl Sandburg.

- Animator Walt Disney introduces sound in cartoons in *Steamboat Willie,* featuring Mickey Mouse.

- *May 11:* Regular television programming is begun on WGY in Schenectady, New York.

- *May 25:* Amelia Earhart becomes the first woman to fly across the Atlantic Ocean.

- *June 12–15:* The Republican National Convention nominates Herbert Hoover and Charles Curtis as candidates for president and vice president.

- *June 26–29:* The Democratic National Convention nominates Alfred E. Smith and Joseph T. Robinson as candidates for president and vice president.

- *July 29–August 12:* The United States wins 24 gold medals at the Summer Olympics in Amsterdam, Holland.

- *July 30:* The first color moving pictures are demonstrated in Rochester, New York.

- *August 27:* In Paris, France, the Kellogg-Briand Peace is agreed to by fifteen nations. The pact calls for outlawing war.

- *October 4–9:* The New York Yankees (AL) defeat the St. Louis Cardinals (NL) to win the World Series.

■ *November 6:* Republicans Herbert Hoover and Charles Curtis defeat Democrats Alfred E. Smith and Joseph T. Robinson and are elected president and vice president.

1929

■ Notable novels include *Sartoris* by William Faulkner, *The Dain Curse* by Dashiell Hammett, *A Farewell to Arms* by Ernest Hemingway, *Laughing Boy* by Oliver La Farge, and *Look Homeward, Angel* by Thomas Wolfe.

■ *January 15:* The Senate passes the Kellogg-Briand Pact.

■ *February 14:* Five gang members (possibly members of Al Capone's gang) gun down seven members of the George "Bugs" Moran gang in Chicago. The event becomes known as the St. Valentine's Day Massacre.

■ *September:* Common stock prices are at record highs.

■ *September:* Sixty percent of Americans make less than $2,000 per year, which is the lowest amount of money the government considers necessary for subsistence.

■ *September 3:* The New York stock market reaches its highest level in history to date.

■ *October 8–14:* The Philadelphia Athletics (AL) defeat the Chicago Cubs (NL) to win the World Series.

■ *October 25:* Former secretary of the Interior Albert Fall is found guilty of accepting a bribe and is sentenced to one year in prison and fined $100,000.

■ *October 29:* Stocks crash. A record number of stocks on the New York Stock Exchange trade: 16,410,030 shares. Much stock is sold for whatever price it will bring, no matter how low. The event is known as Black Tuesday.

On November 13, 1929, stocks on the New York market reached their lowest levels. The *New York Times* listing of the 50 leading stocks showed a loss of about half their value. General Electric went from $396\frac{1}{2}$ to $168\frac{1}{8}$; General Motors went from $72\frac{1}{2}$ to 36.

"Reach for a Lucky instead of a sweet."
—American Tobacco Company slogan for Lucky Strike cigarettes, mid-1920s

CHAPTER 4

1930–1939

I N 1930, 25 PERCENT OF AMERICANS WERE UNEMPLOYED, AND hundreds of banks closed because they ran out of money. Nevertheless, President Herbert Hoover proclaimed that "Business and industry have turned the corner." Voters responded in 1932 by electing a president who promised a "new deal," Democrat Franklin Delano Roosevelt. A distant relative of President Theodore Roosevelt, Franklin Roosevelt implemented his New Deal through a sweeping array of programs. The changes reimagined government as a source of regulatory agencies, laws to protect investors, and public jobs programs. Among the creations were the Federal Deposit Insurance Corporation (FDIC), the Tennessee Valley Authority (TVA), and the Civilian Conservation Corps (CCC). Later, he created the Works Progress Administration (WPA), responsible for building the Lincoln Tunnel and Hoover Dam, among other public works. President Roosevelt's most lasting initiative was Social Security, implemented in 1935. By 1939, the nation and the president turned their attention to the war in Europe, between the Axis powers of Germany, Italy, and Japan, and the Allies of Britain, France, and others. Spectacular movies such as *Gone With the Wind,* exciting baseball stars, and a wide range of radio programming provided diversions along the way.

"Can you not find a quicker way of Executing us than to Starve us to death?"

—letter from New Jersey resident to President Herbert Hoover on deprivations of the depression, 1930

1930

▪ According to the U.S. Census, the population is 122,775,046.

▪ The illiteracy rate in the United States is at its lowest level, 4.3 percent.

▪ Notable novels published include *The 42nd Parallel* by John Dos Passos, *As I Lay Dying* by William Faulkner, *The Maltese Falcon* by Dashiell Hammett, and *Cimarron* by Edna Ferber; poetry published includes *Collected Poems* by Robert Frost and *The Bridge* by Hart Crane.

▪ *March 22:* In the Teapot Dome trial at the Supreme Court in Washington, D.C, Edward Doheny is acquitted.

▪ *May 9:* Gallant Fox wins the 55th annual Preakness Stakes in Baltimore.

- *May 17:* Gallant Fox wins the 56th annual Kentucky Derby.

- *June 7:* Gallant Fox wins the Belmont Stakes in New York and becomes the second horse to win the Triple Crown of horseracing.

- *June 17:* Presient Herbert Hoover signs the protectionist Smoot-Hawley Act into law. It raises duties on nearly 900 articles imported from overseas.

- *August 11:* The American Lutheran Church is formed in Toledo, Ohio.

- *October 1-8:* The Philadelphia Athletics (AL) defeat the St. Louis Cardinals (NL) to win the World Series.

- *October 30:* Dr. Karl Landsteiner of the Rockefeller Institute is the first American to win the Nobel Prize in Physiology or Medicine.

- *November 5:* Sinclair Lewis is the first American to win the Nobel Prize in Literature, for his novel *Babbitt*.

- *November 17:* Golfer Robert "Bobby" Jones Jr. announces his retirement, after setting records and winning 13 of the 27 championship tournaments he entered.

- *December 11:* The Bank of New York, in New York City, closes. It joins the more than 1,200 banks that have already closed due since October 1929.

1931

- Gangster Alphonse "Al" Capone is indicted for income tax evasion.

- Deuterium, or heavy hydrogen, is discovered by Columbia University professor Harold Urey and others. It is important to the development of the atomic bomb.

- Gold hoarding begins as the financial condition of the United States weakens.

In the early 1930s, President Herbert Hoover believed that public relations could help reduce the gloom of the economic disaster that had started in 1929. He began referring to economic collapse as a "depression" to make it sound less scary than "panic."

"Anyone who hates children and dogs can't be all bad."
—William Claude (W. C.) Fields, attributed, 1930s

Al Capone eventually went to jail for not paying his taxes.
(Library of Congress)

As the depression grew worse, the poorest Americans had no money for food. Many stood in breadlines for hours for a free meal. *(Franklin D. Roosevelt Presidential Library and Museum)*

A popular schoolyard rhyme during the depression was: "[Andrew] Mellon pulled the whistle Hoover rang the bell Wall Street gave the signal And the country went to h-ll."

- Notable novels include *The Good Earth* by Pearl S. Buck, *Shadows on the Rock* by Willa Cather, *Sanctuary* by William Faulkner, and *The Forge* by T. S. Stribling; notable poetry includes *ViVa* by e.e. cummings.

- *January 7:* Unemployment rates range between 4 million and 5 million.

- *January 19:* The National Commission on Law Observance and Law Enforcement issues a report on the state of enforcement of antiliquor laws. It recommends that enforcement be done by federal government.

- *March 3:* President Herbert Hoover signs an act making "The Star-Spangled Banner" by Francis Scott Key the national anthem.

- *May 1:* The Empire State Building opens in New York City. It is the tallest building in the world at the time.

- *June 23:* From New York, aviators Wiley Post and Harold Gatty begin a flight around the world.

- *July 1:* Wiley Post and Harold Gatty complete their round-the-world flight, back in New York.

- *September:* A widespread bank panic occurs across the nation. It results in 305 bank closings.

- *October:* The bank panic continues. During the month, 522 banks close nationwide.

- *October 1–10:* The St. Louis Cardinals (NL) defeat the Philadelphia Athletics (AL) to win the World Series.

- *October 17:* Al Capone is convicted of income tax evasion and sentenced to 11 years in prison.

1932

- Unemployment numbers in the nation range between 11 and 13 million. Those working have wages that are 60 percent less than they were in 1929.

- Losses for business across the nation range between five billion and six billion dollars. Overall, industry in the United States is operating at less than half its 1929 top rate.

- President Herbert Hoover approves the five-day workweek for most government employees.

- Notable popular music includes the song "Brother, Can You Spare a Dime?" by E. Y. "Yip" Harburg.

- Notable novels include *Tobacco Road* by Erskine Caldwell, *1919* by John Dos Passos, *Light in August* by William Faulkner, and *The Store* by T. S. Stribling; notable plays include *The Animal Kingdom* by Phillip Barry.

- *February 4–13:* At the Winter Olympics in Lake Placid, New York, the U.S. team wins ten gold medals. It is the first time an Olympics is held in the United States.

- *March 1:* Charles A. Lindbergh Jr., 20 months old, is kidnapped from his family's house in Hopewell, New Jersey.

The Empire State Building, completed in 1931, is one of the most recognizable landmarks on the New York City skyline. *(Library of Congress)*

> **T**he depression affected children greatly. The New York City Health Department reported that in 1932, 20 percent of its public schoolchildren were suffering from malnutrition.

Roosevelt was an effective campaigner. During the 1932 campaign, he often stopped to speak personally to American voters, listening to their problems. *(Library of Congress)*

The Lindbergh kidnapping arouses immediate media and law enforcement attention.

- *May 12:* The body of Charles Lindbergh Jr. is located, after a $50,000 ransom is paid.

- *May 20:* Amelia Earhart is the first woman to fly a plane solo across the Atlantic Ocean.

- *May 29:* About 1,000 former servicemen known as the Bonus Army arrive in Washington, D.C., seeking payment of their veterans' bonus certificates.

- *June:* Up to 16,000 additional servicemen join the initial Bonus Army members in Washington, D.C., seeking reimbursement. They set up camp in unused buildings and self-constructed housing.

- *July:* Many Bonus Army members are paid by the government and enticed to leave their Washington encampment.

- *June 27–July 2:* Franklin Delano Roosevelt and John Nance Garner are nominated as presidential and vice-presidential candidates at the Democratic National Convention, defeating New York governor Al Smith.

- *July 2:* Democratic presidential nominee Franklin Roosevelt officially introduces the term *New Deal* to describe his political platform and plan for the future for Americans.

- *July 28:* The 2,000 Bonus Army members who remain camped in Washington, D.C., are driven out by troops led by Gen. Douglas MacArthur.

- *July 30–August 14:* At the Summer Olympics in Los Angeles, California, the U.S. wins 16 gold medals.

- *September 4:* Olin Duta wins the PGA golf tournament.

- *September 28–October 2:* The New York Yankees (AL) defeat the Chicago Cubs (NL) to win the World Series.

- *November 8:* Democrat Franklin Delano Roosevelt defeats Republican President Herbert Hoover to become president.

In a landslide election, Roosevelt carries 41 states; the electoral vote is 472 to 59.

1933

- Life expectancy of the average American is 59 years.

- Nationwide, more than 2 million children no longer attend school due to economic insecurity. More than 200,000 teachers nationwide are unemployed.

- The American Federation of Labor has 4 million members.

- The positron, or positively charged electron, is discovered by physicists.

- The government-sponsored Civil Works Administration begins to commission many dozens of artists and architects to design and provide murals for public buildiings.

- Notable movies include *Little Women* and *She Done Him Wrong.*

- Notable novels include *Anthony Adverse* by Hervey Allen, *God's Little Acre* by Erskine Caldwell, and *Winner Take Nothing* by Ernest Hemingway. Other literary works include *The Autobiography of Alice B. Toklas* by Gertrude Stein.

- *February 6:* The Twentieth Amendment to the Constitution is adopted. It shifts the presidential inauguration date to January 20 from March 4. It also provides a succession procedure allowing for the vice president to assume the presidency upon the death of the president-elect.

- *March 1:* Bank holidays begin to be established to quell panics among consumers. On this day holidays are established in six states.

- *March 4:* Franklin D. Roosevelt is inaugurated as president. He delivers an inaugural address proclaiming, "The only thing we have to fear is fear itself."

- *March 4:* Frances Perkins is appointed secretary of labor, becoming the first woman to hold a Cabinet position.

In 1932, when the U.S. Army burned housing set up by World War I veterans (the so-called Bonus Army) who were fighting for promised war bonuses, the public had little sympathy. They thought the squatters were freeloaders, not deserving veterans. But the Veterans' Administration catalogued that 94 percent of the inhabitants were World War I veterans.

"The only thing we have to fear is fear itself."

—Franklin Delano Roosevelt, First Inaugural Address, March 4, 1933

President Hoover (left) accompanied president-elect Roosevelt (right) to his 1933 inauguration. The two had become bitter rivals, and Hoover refused to speak to Roosevelt on the ride. *(Library of Congress)*

■ *March 12:* President Roosevelt holds his first fireside chat, a topical radio speech.

■ *March 13:* Banks begin to reopen across the country following a widespread bank panic.

■ *March 31:* The Civilian Conservation Corps (CCC) is begun.

■ *May 12:* The Agricultural Adjustment Act (AAA) takes effect, regulating crop production and paying bounties to farmers for reduced production.

■ *May 18:* The Tennessee Valley Act is passed, setting up the Tennessee Valley Authority (TVA), to build dams that will power electrical plants and regulate floods in the area.

■ *May 27–November 2:* The Century of Progress Exposition is held in Chicago, Illinois, celebrating Chicago's founding.

■ *June 16:* The National Industrial Recovery Act (NIR) is created. It sets up the National Recovery Administration (NRA) and the Pubic Works Administration (PWA).

■ *June 16:* The Banking Act of 1933 is passed. It establishes the Federal Bank Deposit Insurance Corporation.

■ *October 3–7:* The New York Giants (NL) defeat the Washington Senators (AL) to win the World Series.

"Why don't you come up sometime and see me?"

—Mae West, *She Done Him Wrong,* screenplay, 1933

- *October 20:* Scientist Thomas Hunt Morgan is awarded the Novel Prize in Physiology or Medicine for his research on chromosomes and their effect on heredity.

- *November 8:* The Civil Works Administration is established to provide work for up to 4 million unemployed Americans. Harry Hopkins is the administration's first director.

- *December 5:* Prohibition is repealed as the Twenty-first Amendment to the Constitution is ratified by Utah.

- *December 6:* The ban on the novel *Ulysses* by James Joyce is removed by Federal Judge John M. Woolsey.

- *December 17:* The first National Football League (NFL) championship playoff is held, and the Chicago Bears defeat the New York Giants.

1934

- Unemployment drops by more than 4 million.

- By the end of the year, 33 new government agencies will have been created.

- At 58, the number of bank closings is greatly reduced from hundreds of annual closings in the past decade.

- The American Federation of Labor has 2 million new members.

- Alcohol distillers produce 35 million barrels of beer and 42 million gallons of hard liquor.

- Notable movies include *It Happened One Night* and *The Gay Divorcee.*

- Notable novels include *Tender Is the Night* by F. Scott Fitzgerald, *The Thin Man* by Dashiell Hammett, and *Goodbye, Mr. Chips* by James Hilton.

- *March 24:* Congress passes the Tydings-McDuffie Act, which grants independence to the Philippines.

CCC workers clear dead wood from Sequoia National Park in California. *(Franklin D. Roosevelt Presidential Library and Museum)*

Shirley Temple won an Academy Award in 1934 for her "outstanding contribution to film." Here, she celebrates a birthday with another Hollywood star, Eddie Cantor. *(Library of Congress)*

President Roosevelt delivers one of his fireside chats on radio. He was the first president to use the media to appeal directly to the public. *(AP/Wide World)*

"I joked about every prominent man in my lifetime, but I never met one I didn't like."

—Will Rogers, epitaph, 1935

■ *May 23:* The synthetic fiber now known as nylon is produced at the Du Pont laboratories. Its initial name is polymer 66.

■ *June 6:* President Roosevelt signs the Securities Exchange Act, helping create the Securities and Exchange Commission.

■ *June 14:* Max Baer defeats Primo Carnera to win the world heavyweight boxing championship,

■ *June 28:* Congress passes the National Housing Act, which establishes the Federal Housing Administration, an advocacy government organization.

■ *June 28:* President Roosevelt signs the Federal Farm Bankruptcy Act, which indefinitely ends foreclosures on farms.

■ *July 16:* The first general strike in U.S. history occurs in San Francisco, California.

■ *July 22:* Gangster John Dillinger is shot by FBI agents near a Chicago movie house.

- *July 29:* Paul Runyan wins the PGA golf tournament.

- *October 3–9:* The St. Louis Cardinals (NL) defeat the Detroit Tigers (AL) to win the World Series.

- *December 9:* The New York Giants defeat the Chicago Bears to win the NFL championship.

1935

- An epidemic of polio, also called infantile paralysis, strikes nationwide.

- Notable movies include *The Informer* and *A Tale of Two Cities.*

- Notable books include *Tortilla Flat* by John Steinbeck, *Judgement Day* by James T. Farrell, and *Of Time and the River* by Thomas Wolfe

- *January 29:* The Senate rejects U.S. membership in the World Court.

- *April 8:* The Emergency Relief Appropriation Act is adopted.

- *May 4–June 8:* Omaha wins the Kentucky Derby, the Preakness Stakes, and the Belmont Stakes, becoming the third horse to win the Triple Crown.

- *May 6:* The Works Progress Administration (WPA) is instituted under the provisions of the Emergency Relief Appropriation Act.

- *May 11:* A presidential executive order establishes the Rural Electrification Administration, which aims to build power sources for areas without electric power.

- *May 24:* The first night baseball game in the major leagues is played.

- *May 27:* The Supreme Court declares the National Industrial Recovery Act unconstitutional. The decision makes the National Recovery Administration, (NRA), which

The WPA included projects for those with special skills like teachers and artists. This poster announces a WPA arts and crafts exhibit in New York. *(Library of Congress)*

America's first parking meters went into service in Oklahoma City, Oklahoma, in 1935. The meters cut down on traffic and raised money for the city government. Cars park along the "new" parking meters in Omaha, Nebraska, in 1938. *(Library of Congress)*

MORE SECURITY FOR THE AMERICAN FAMILY

THE SOCIAL SECURITY ACT AS AMENDED OFFERS GREATER OLD-AGE INSURANCE PROTECTION TO PEOPLE NOW NEARING RETIREMENT AGE.

FOR INFORMATION WRITE OR CALL AT THE NEAREST FIELD OFFICE OF THE **SOCIAL SECURITY BOARD**

Many states reacted to the poverty of the early depression with their own old-age pension programs. The national Social Security law was passed in 1935. *(Franklin D. Roosevelt Presidential Library and Museum)*

"There is only one way under high Heaven to get anybody to do anything.... And that is by making the other person want to do it."

—Dale Carnegie, *How to Win Friends and Influence People*, 1936

attempted to regulate prices and other working conditions, invalid.

- *June 10:* Alcoholics Anonymous is founded in New York City. Its leader is Bill W.

- *July 6:* Helen Wills Moody wins the women's singles championships at Wimbledon.

- *August 14:* President Roosevelt signs the Social Security Act. This program of old-age benefits collects a percentage from workers' earnings that will go toward payments to them once they reach 65 years of age.

- *August 16:* Humorist Will Rogers dies with aviator Wiley Post in an airplane crash in Alaska.

- *September 8:* Louisiana politician Huey Long is assassinated in Baton Rouge, Louisiana, by Dr. Carl Weiss, Jr.

- *October 2–7:* The Detroit Tigers (AL) defeat the Chicago Cubs (NL) to win the World Series.

- *November 9:* Labor leader John L. Lewis breaks from the American Federation of Labor to found another union, the Committee for Industrial Organization.

- *December 15:* The Detroit Lions defeat the New York Giants, 15–7, to win the NFL championship.

1936

- Eight million Americans remain unemployed.

- A drought in Midwest and Great Plains area of the United States creates a dust bowl that destroys crops and land. Thousands head west, looking for work.

- Germany reclaims and reoccupies the Rhineland.

- Italy annexes Ethiopia.

- Civil war begins in Spain.

- Notable movies include *Mr. Deeds Goes to Town* and *The Great Ziegfeld.*

- Notable novels include *Gone With the Wind* by Margaret Mitchell and *The Big Money* by John Dos Passos; poetry includes *A Further Range* by Robert Frost.

- *January 6:* The U.S. Supreme Court rules the Agricultural Adjustment Act invalid.

- *March 2:* President Roosevelt signs the Soil Conservation and Domestic Allotment Act, for farmers.

- *May 9:* The *Hindenberg* lands in Lakehurst, New Jersey, making it the first transatlantic dirigible traveling on schedule.

- *August 5–16:* At the Summer Olympics in Berlin, the United States wins 20 gold medals. Four are won by African-American runner Jesse Owens.

- *September 30–October 6:* The New York Yankees (AL) defeat the New York Giants (NL) to win the World Series.

- *November 3:* Democrat Franklin Roosevelt is re-elected president of the United States in a landslide victory.

- *November 22:* Denny Shute wins the PGA golf tournament.

> **"Frankly, my dear, I don't give a damn."**
>
> —Margaret Mitchell, *Gone with the Wind,* Rhett Butler to Scarlett O'Hara, 1936

> **"This is terrible! This is one of the worst catastrophes in the world! Oh the humanity and all the passengers."**
>
> —Radio announcer Herbert Morrison describing the crash of the airship *Hindenberg,* May 6, 1937

Jesse Owens won four gold medals in the 1936 Olympics. In each event, Owens either tied or set new Olympic records. *(Library of Congress)*

Dance marathons were eventually banned in most areas due to the risks to the dancers' lives. *(Granger Collection)*

In 1937, the average American family of four was still not out of the depression. The average yearly total for that four was $1,348; 98 percent lived on less than $5,000 per year. Big earners such as Louis B. Mayer, head of MGM, had a yearly salary of $1,161,753.

1937

▪ Hundreds of Americans volunteer to fight with the Loyalist army in Spain during the Spanish Civil War.

▪ Notable movies include *Camille* and *Snow White and the Seven Dwarfs.*

▪ Notable novels include *The Late George Apley* by John P. Marquand and *Of Mice and Men* by John Steinbeck.

▪ *February 5:* President Roosevelt informs Congress of his wish to revise rules for installing federal judges. Many politicians and the public see the revisions as an attempt to pack the Supreme Court with justices more favorable to President Roosevelt and his policies.

▪ *April 12:* The Supreme Court upholds the National Labor Relations Act of 1935.

▪ *May 6:* The dirigible *Hindenburg* bursts into flames while mooring at Lakehurst, New Jersey. The crash brings on the end of dirigible travel.

- *May 8–June 5:* War Admiral becomes the fourth horse on record to win the Triple Crown.

- *May 12:* The coronation of King George VI of England marks the first radio broadcast carried worldwide.

- *May 27:* The Golden Gate Bridge in San Francisco is dedicated.

- *May 30:* Denny Shute wins the PGA golf tournament.

- *June 12:* Ralph Guldahl wins the U.S. Open golf tournament.

- *June 22:* Joe Louis defeats James J. Braddock to win the world heavyweight boxing championship.

- *August 12:* President Roosevelt appoints Hugo L. Black to the Supreme Court.

- *September 2:* President Roosevelt signs the National Housing Act. Also known as the Wagner-Seagall Act, it creates the U.S. Housing Authority, which admimisters small-scale loans.

- *October 6–10:* The New York Yankees (AL) defeat the New York Giants (NL) to win the World Series.

1938

- Ten million fans attend major-league baseball games this year.

- Notable plays include *Our Town* by Thornton Wilder and *The Fifth Column* by Ernest Hemingway.

- Notable movies include *Boys Town* and *Angels with Dirty Faces.*

- Notable novels include *The Unvanquished* by William Faulkner and *Black is My Truelove's Hair* by Elizabeth Madox Roberts; poetry includes *Land of the Free* by Archibald MacLeish.

A worker looks out from the north tower of the Golden Gate Bridge during construction.
(Library of Congress)

> *"[L]ook, up there in the sky, it's a bird, it's a plane, it's Superman!"*
>
> —Jerry Siegel and Joe Shuster, Superman, comic strip, 1938

Joe Louis knocks out Max Schmeling in the first round of their rematch in 1938. Louis was heavyweight champion 1937–49, longer than any other boxer. (AP/Wide World)

In one of the dust storms over the Midwest and Great Plains during the mid-1930s, some 300 million tons of top soil was lifted from the farms of the southern plains. That was as much earth as had been dredged to build the Panama Canal.

■ *March:* The economic stock recession is at its worst in years. Major stocks drop precipitously in value.

■ *April 10:* Germany annexes and occupies Austria.

■ *May 26:* The Committee to Investigate Un-American Activities (HUAC) is formed to monitor potentially dangerous groups.

■ *May 27:* Congress passes the Revenue Bill of 1938, which offers tax cuts to big corporations.

■ *June 23:* Congress passes the Civil Aeronautics Act, which establishes the Civil Aeronautics Authority to provide independent regulation of pilots, flights, and equipment.

■ *June 25:* President Roosevelt signs the Wage and Hours Act, which raises the minimum wage for workers engaged in interstate commerce from 25 to 40 cents per hour. It also regulates workers' hours per week.

■ *July 17:* Douglas G. "Wrong Way" Corrigan flies from New York to Dublin, Ireland, insisting when he landed that all the time he had meant to go to California.

■ *September 26:* President Roosevelt sends private memorandums to Britain, France, Germany, and Czechoslovakia about international conflicts.

■ *September 29:* The Munich Pact is enacted, enlarging Germany's power in Europe.

■ *October 5–9:* The New York Yankees (AL) defeat the Chicago Cubs (NL) to win the World Series in four straight games.

■ *October 30:* Actor Orson Welles's radio play of H. G. Wells's *War of the Worlds* generates national alarm when listeners believe the false news reports of alien invasion to be true.

■ *November 14–18:* The Congress of Industrial Organizations (CIO) is set up at the meeting of the Committee or Industrial Organization. John L. Lewis is elected president.

ALAN LOMAX

Beginning in 1933, Alan Lomax traveled with his father throughout the United States making field recordings of traditional American folk music for the Library of Congress Archive of Folk Song. Much of this music was blues and jazz played by African-American musicians ignored by the music industry, including Leadbelly and Muddy Waters, and unknown to white America. In 1938, Lomax recorded several hours of Jelly Roll Morton, whom many regard as one of the creators of jazz.

By 1939, Lomax was bringing this music to the public on his weekly CBS radio series called *American Folk Song,* where he also introduced such important white folksingers as Woody Guthrie and Pete Seeger. The recordings Lomax made had a tremendous influence on American and, later, British popular music. Everyone from rock 'n' rollers of the 1950s to Bob Dylan in the 1960s to Led Zeppelin and Eric Clapton in the 1970s turned to Lomax's recordings for inspiration and ideas.

Alan Lomax (above) performs at a concert in Asheville, North Carolina. *(Library of Congress)*

■ *December 11:* The New York Giants defeat the Green Bay Packers to win the NFL championship.

■ *December 13:* The Works Progress Administration submits a report announcing that unemployment levels have dropped significantly, to 2,122,960. In 1937, the number was 3,184,000.

1939

■ World fairs are held in New York City and San Francisco, each one heralding the great developments of the future.

■ Scientists announce that the atom has been split in a laboratory by bombardment with neutrons.

■ Frequency modulation (FM), a form of radio transmission, is developed by Edwin Armstrong.

■ Notable movies include *Stagecoach, Mr. Smith Goes to Washington,* and the blockbuster Civil War drama *Gone with the Wind.* It gains immediate critical acclaim and breaks box-office records.

"Somewhere over the rainbow...."

—Edgar Y. Harburg, *The Wizard of Oz,* Over the Rainbow, 1939

In 1939, opera sensation Marian Anderson was scheduled to sing at Constitution Hall, which belonged to the Daughters of the American Revolution. When they refused to allow her to appear because she was an African American, First Lady Eleanor Roosevelt set up a free outdoor concert featuring Anderson on the steps of the Lincoln Memorial instead. *(Library of Congress)*

- Notable novels include *The Grapes of Wrath* by John Steinbeck and *The Wild Palms* by William Faulkner; notable nonfiction includes *Abraham Lincoln: The War Years* by Carl Sandburg; poetry includes *Collected Poems* by Robert Frost and *Collected Poems* by Mark Van Doren.

- *June 8:* King George VI and Queen Elizabeth arrive in Washington, D.C., becoming the first British sovereigns to visit the United States.

- *June 28:* Regularly scheduled transatlantic air transportation begins with a Pan American flight from Long Island to Portugal.

- *August:* Russia and Germany sign a nonaggression pact.

- *September 1:* Germany invades Poland but does not declare war.

- *September 3:* France and Great Britain declare war on Germany.

- *September 3:* President Roosevelt makes a fireside chat declaring the United States's neutrality.

- *September 3:* The British passenger ship *Athenia* is sunk by a submarine. Thirty Americans aboard are killed.

- *October 4–8:* The New York Yankees (AL) defeat the Cincinnati Reds (NL) to win the World Series.

- *October 18:* President Roosevelt signs an executive order closing all United States ports and waters to enemy submarines.

- *November 4:* Congress passes the Neutrality Act of 1939, which permits arms to be exported and allows the sale of arms to warring powers.

CHAPTER 5

1940–1949

T HE DECADE BEGAN WITH THE ELECTION OF FRANKLIN ROOSEVELT TO A third term. The morning surprise attack on December 7, 1941, by the Japanese at Pearl Harbor ended U.S. isolationism. On December 8, 1941, President Roosevelt called December 7 "a day which will live in infamy," and Congress voted to declare war on Japan. On December 11, the United States entered the war with Germany and Italy. The U.S.-led Allied D-Day invasion at Normandy on June 6, 1944, was followed by the liberation of Europe and V-E, or Victory in Europe Day, on May 8, 1945. The victory arrived too late for commander-in-chief President Roosevelt, who died in April 1945. On August 6, 1945, the *Enola Gay* dropped an atomic bomb on Hiroshima, Japan. On August 9, another was dropped, on Nagasaki. Several days later, Japan surrendered, and World War II was over. Postwar, the United States administered a massive European aid program, the Marshall Plan. Meanwhile, in the United States, British prime minister Winston Churchill spoke about the existence of an "iron curtain" separating communist and free nations. Most Americans were more concerned about everyday problems, such as finding a house in the suburbs.

1940

- The population of the United States is 131,669,275, according to the 1940 Census.

- The average life expectancy of Americans is 64 years.

- Because of world war, the 1940 Olympic Games are not held. Neither are the Davis Cup and Wimbledon matches.

- Notable novels published include *The Hamlet* by William Faulkner, *For Whom the Bell Tolls* by Ernest Hemingway, and *You Can't Go Home Again* by Thomas Wolfe.

- *September 16:* Congress passes the Selective Service Act, creating the first national peacetime draft.

- *October 2–8:* The Cincinnati Reds (NL) defeat the Detroit Tigers (AL) to win the World Series.

- *October 24:* The 40-hour workweek becomes law as the Fair Labor Standards Act of 1938 is enacted.

"We must be the great arsenal of democracy."

—Franklin Delano Roosevelt, in a fireside chat radio broadcast, December 29, 1940

President Franklin Roosevelt appears on the cover of *Look* magazine, in a photo taken in Warm Springs, Georgia, in 1939. Roosevelt's calm and confident leadership helped the nation endure years of economic depression and world war. *(Library of Congress)*

- *November 5:* Franklin Roosevelt is elected president for a third term. Henry Wallace is the vice president.

1941

- An embargo on Japanese silk imports suspends hosiery manufacture in the United States, leading to a rush to buy whatever stock remains on store shelves. A synthetic fiber, rayon, is eventually substituted but proves much inferior.

- *January 20:* Franklin D. Roosevelt is inaugurated president and Henry Wallace is inaugurated vice president.

- *March 1:* President Franklin Roosevelt signs the Lend-Lease Bill.

- *April 11:* The Office of Price Administration and Civilian Supply (known as OPA) is established.

- *May 3–June 7:* Whirlaway wins the Kentucky Derby, the Preakness Stakes, and the Belmont Stakes, winning the Triple Crown of horseracing.

- *June 22:* Germany invades the Soviet Union.

- *July 17:* Yankee centerfielder Joe DiMaggio ends his record-setting hitting streak of 56 consecutive games.

- *August 9–12:* President Franklin Roosevelt and British prime minister Winston Churchill secretly create the Atlantic Charter, which outlines their aims.

- *October 1–6:* The New York Yankees (AL) defeat the Brooklyn Dodgers (NL) in the World Series.

- *October 30:* The U.S. destroyer *Reuben James* is sunk near Iceland by a German submarine. About 100 Americans die.

- *December 7:* The U.S. military base at Pearl Harbor, Hawaii, is attacked by Japanese forces. About 19 U.S. ships are destroyed or damaged. Approximately 3,000 Americans die. At the same time, Japan attacks Guam, the Philippines, and Wake Island.

NYLON, THE MIRACLE FIBER

There were no pantyhose in 1940. Women wore stockings, one for each leg, held up with garters attached to a belt worn under their clothes. The best hose were knitted of silk, on complex machines, and sewn together with a tiny seam in the back.

The Du Pont chemical company had developed nylon and introduced it to the public on October 28, 1938. Their press release claimed: "Though wholly fabricated from such common raw materials as coal, water and air, nylon can be fashioned into filaments strong as steel, as fine as the spider's web...." Du Pont specifically intended the consumer material for women's hose. The name came from New York (ny) and London (lon), two cities where Du Pont thought the item would be particularly popular.

But women everywhere went wild for the new nylon stockings, which lasted longer, looked more attractive, and fit better than silk. When nylon stockings first went on sale, in May 1940, stores nationwide sold out immediately. But to many women's horror, the hose were suddenly snatched away. The War Production Board decreed that all nylon production had to be devoted to the war effort, for parachutes and tires. Silk, too, was used for parachutes and was in short supply.

One woman wrote in an October 1942 issue of *Business Week* magazine: "Women were given a glorified hose several years ago, and that is what they want now. Nylon hose came, conquered and disappeared with a short time and now the women are rebelling good and strong...These substitutes which are being thrust upon us this fall are horrible, last no time and certainly don't look as good as nylon."

A thriving black market existed for nylon stockings, but because the only legitimate buyer of nylon was the U.S. government, most items on the black market were fakes. Many women wound up paying $10 a pair for cheap, inferior rayon stockings labeled "nylon" or using eyeliner to draw a mock seam on the back of their bare legs.

- *December 8:* Congress passes a declaration of war against Japan.

- *December 10:* Japan attacks U.S. and Philippine forces and invades the Phillipines at Luzon.

- *December 11:* Germany and Italy declare war on the United States. Congress passes a resolution of war against both nations.

- *December 27:* The OPA initiates rubber rationing.

1942

- Notable books include *The Moonlit Down* by John Steinbeck, *The Robe* by Lloyd C. Douglas, and *See Here, Private Hargrove* by Marion Hargrove.

- *January 2:* U.S. and Philippine forces lose Manila to the Japanese. Allied forces retreat to Bataan.

In an underground tunnel, British soldiers stack cases of U.S.-made explosives. *(Library of Congress)*

"I shall return."

—Douglas MacArthur, on arriving in Australia from the Philippines, March 30, 1942

A popular slogan for Americans during rationing was, "Use it up, wear it out, make it do, or do without."

■ *February 27–March 1:* Japanese naval forces defeat U.S. forces in the Battle of the Java Sea.

■ *March 17:* U.S. commander Douglas MacArthur leaves Bataan and becomes commander-in-chief of the Southwest Pacific Command.

■ *April 10:* American and Philippine prisoners of the Japanese begin the Bataan Death March. They are forced to walk 85 miles in six days with one meal of rice per day. On the march, more than 5,000 prisoners die.

■ *May 6:* Japanese forces defeat U.S. forces at Corregidor.

■ *May 5:* Sugar rationing begins in the United States.

■ *June 4–6:* U.S. forces score a decisive victory against Japanese forces at the Battle of Midway.

■ *August–February:* U.S. amphibious forces enter Guadalcanal, beginning a bloody long-term battle.

■ *September 30–October 5:* The St. Louis Cardinals (NL) defeat the New York Yankees (AL) to win the World Series.

■ *November 7:* U.S. and British forces land in North Africa.

■ *November 12–15:* U.S. naval forces fight to victory against Japanese forces at Guadalcanal.

■ *November 29:* Coffee rationing begins.

■ *December 1:* Gasoline rationing begins nationwide.

■ *December 2:* Scientists set up and observe the first sustained nuclear reaction at the University of Chicago.

1943

■ A polio epidemic strikes the United States, killing 1,151 and disabling thousands more.

JOLTIN' JOE'S STREAK

In the summer of 1941, baseball fans watched breathlessly as Joe DiMaggio of the New York Yankees went on one of sports history's greatest winning streaks. From May 15 to July 17, the Yankee Clipper hit safely in 56 games in a row, until the Cleveland Indians managed to keep him off base in front of a crowd of more than 67,000. (The Yankees managed to win the game 4-3 anyway.) DiMaggio's streak shattered the previous record for hitting safely by 15 games, and his record still stands untouched as of 2005.

Joe Dimaggio helped the Yankees win ten pennants and nine World Series from 1936 to 1951. He served in the U.S. Army from 1943 through 1945. *(National Baseball Hall of Fame Library and Museum)*

■ The United States begins large-scale manufacture of the antibiotic drug penicillin.

■ The jitterbug, a fast swing dance, is popular.

■ American clothing designers emerge as fashion trendsetters in the United States, taking the place of French designers.

■ The innovative Broadway musical *Oklahoma!* by Richard Rodgers and Oscar Hammerstein II opens.

■ Notable literary works include *Thirty Seconds Over Tokyo* by Capt. Ted Lawson, *The Human Comedy* by William Saroyan, *God Is My Co-Pilot* by Colonel Robert Scott Jr., and *A Tree Grows in Brooklyn* by Betty Smith.

"There's a tree that grows in Brooklyn. Some people call it the Tree of Heaven."

—Betty Smith, *A Tree Grows in Brooklyn,* 1943

This poster advertised the original 1943 production of *Oklahoma!* *(Library of Congress)*

- *February 7:* Shoe rationing, which allows the purchase of three pairs of shoes per year, begins.

- *March:* Rationing of canned goods, cheese, fat, and meat begins.

- *May 1–June 5:* Count Fleet wins the Kentucky Derby, the Preakness Stakes, and the Belmont Stakes, earning the Triple Crown.

- *May 5:* Postmaster General Frank Walker announces a zip code numbering system for cities.

- *May 12:* The campaign in North Africa ends.

- *May 25:* Race riots break out in Mobile, Alabama.

- *June 4:* Race riots take place in Los Angeles, California.

- *June 14:* The Supreme Court rules in a case involving Jehovah's Witnesses that schoolchildren do not have to salute the flag if doing so goes against their religion.

- *June 19:* Race riots take place in Beaumont, Texas.

- *June 20–22:* Race riots occur in Detroit, Michigan, often involving individuals brought to war plants to work. Thirty-five people are killed, 500 wounded.

- *July:* Allied forces invade Sicily and bomb Rome.

- *August 1:* Race riots break out in Harlem, New York.

- *August 17:* Allied forces conquer Sicily.

- *September 3:* Allied forces invade mainland Italy.

- *September 8:* Italy surrenders to Allied forces.

- *October 5–11:* The New York Yankees (AL) defeat the St. Louis Cardinals (NL) in the World Series.

- *October 13:* Italy declares war on Germany.

"Here's looking at you, kid."

—Julius J. Epstein, Philip G. Epstein, and Howard Koch, *Casablanca,* 1943

- *November 28–Dec. 1:* President Franklin Roosevelt, Prime Minister Winston Churchill, and Russian premier Joseph Stalin set Allied strategy at the Teheran conference.

- *December 24:* General Dwight D. Eisenhower is named supreme commander of Allied forces for invading Europe.

1944

- Despite government price controls, the cost of living rises.

- Women join the work force in large numbers as more men are called to war.

- Motion picture revenues reach an all-time high. Bob Hope and Bing Crosby are major box-office draws.

- Notable novels include *A Bell for Adano* by John Hersey and *Strange Fruit* by Lillian Smith.

- *May:* Italy falls to Allied forces.

- *May 3:* Meat rationing ends.

- *June–September:* German forces introduce two new weapons, the V-1, a bomb, and V-2, a supersonic rocket.

- *June 4–5:* Allied forces enter and overtake Rome.

- *June 6:* Allied forces land in Normandy, France, in the massive invasion is known as D-Day. General Dwight D. Eisenhower commands 3,000 planes and 4,000 ships. Four million Allied troops take part.

- *June 16:* U.S. forces begin the Allied bombing of Japan.

- *August 8:* Allied forces take Brittany, and U.S. forces drive on toward Paris.

- *August 9:* Guam falls to U.S. forces.

- *August 21:* The Dumbarton Oaks conference takes place in Washington, D.C. The United States, Great Britain, China,

"Battle is the most magnificent competition in which a human being can indulge."

—General George S. Patton, message to his troops, 1943

Signs like this one were a common sight in the southern states during the 1940s. *(Library of Congress)*

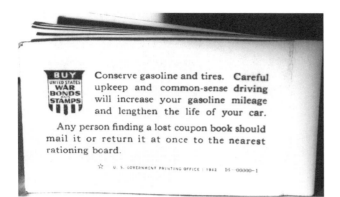

Conserve gasoline and tires. Careful upkeep and common-sense driving will increase your gasoline mileage and lengthen the life of your car.

Any person finding a lost coupon book should mail it or return it at once to the nearest rationing board.

☆ U. S. GOVERNMENT PRINTING OFFICE : 1942 16—00000-1

A ration book from 1944 reminds American civilians of the benefits of wise automobile use. (*Library of Congress*)

"*Good evening, Mr. and Mrs. America and all the ships at sea! This is Walter Winchell in New York.*"

—Walter Winchell's introduction to his weekly radio broadcasts, 1940s

and the Soviet Union discuss creating a postwar organization that will become the United Nations.

- *August 25:* Allied forces liberate Paris.

- *September 12:* U.S. forces enter Germany.

- *October 4–9:* The St. Louis Cardinals (NL) defeat the St. Louis Browns (AL) to win the World Series.

- *October 20:* American forces land in the Philippine Islands at Leyte.

- *October 23–26:* The Battle of Leyte Gulf takes place between the Japanese and U.S. naval forces. It is the largest naval battle of World War II.

- *November 7:* Democrat Franklin D. Roosevelt and Harry S Truman are elected president and vice-president.

- *December 16:* The Battle of the Bulge begins in the Ardennes between German and Allied troops.

1945

- Publishers begin to make books widely available in paperback editions, which increases sales greatly.

- "Kilroy was here" becomes a popular graffiti phrase among U.S. soldiers, who write it throughout the world.

- Notable novels include *Black Boy* by Richard Wright and *Cass Timberlane* by Sinclair Lewis; nonfiction includes *The Age of Jackson* by Arthur M. Schlesinger Jr.

- *January 9:* U.S. troops land in Luzon, Philippines.

- *February 4–11:* President Roosevelt, British prime minister Winston Churchill, and Russian premier Joseph Stalin attend the secret Yalta Conference in Ukraine. They discuss the rebuilding of postwar Europe.

February 23: On Mt. Suribachi at Iwo Jima, U.S. troops raise the American flag.

March 16: Iwo Jima falls to the U.S. Marines.

April 1: U.S. forces invade Okinawa.

April 12: President Franklin D. Roosevelt dies in Warm Spring, Georgia, of a cerebral hemorrhage. He is 63.

April 12: Vice president Harry S Truman becomes president.

May 8: V-E Day marks victory in Europe.

June 21: Japanese forces surrender Okinawa to Allied forces.

June 26: The charter for the United Nations is signed in San Francisco, California.

July 5: General Douglas MacArthur announces that the Philippine Islands have been liberated.

July 16: Scientists detonate the first atomic bomb near Alamogordo, New Mexico.

July 28: The Senate approves the UN Charter. The vote is 89 to 2.

August 6: The United States drops the atomic bomb on Hiroshima, Japan. The city is destroyed.

August 9: The United States drops the atomic bomb on Nagasaki, Japan. The city is destroyed.

August 15: V-J Day marks Allied victory over Japan.

October–December: Rationing ends.

October 3–10: The Detroit Tigers (AL) defeat the Chicago Cubs (NL) to win the World Series.

"Who's on first, What's on second, I Don't Know's on third—"

—Bud Abbott and Lou Costello, *The Naughty Nineties,* 1945

The distinctive mushroom cloud of an atomic explosion rises 60,000 feet into the air over Nagasaki on the morning of August 9, 1945. *(Library of Congress)*

"[W]hat good mothers and fathers instinctively feel like doing for their babies is the best after all."

—Dr. Benjamin Spock,
The Common Sense Book of Baby and Child Care, 1946

The return of so many veterans led to a severe shortage of housing. Here, three vets, attending the University of Wisconsin on the G.I. Bill, camp out in a tent to protest the point. *(Library of Congress)*

■ *December 16:* The Cleveland Rams defeat the Washington Redskins 15 to 14, to win the NFL championship.

1946

■ A housing shortage affects the United States as large numbers of veterans return home.

■ Notable books include novels *Mister Roberts* by Thomas Heggen and *All the King's Men* by Robert Penn Warren; nonfiction includes *The Common Sense Book of Baby and Child Care* by Benjamin Spock.

■ *February 15:* ENIAC (Electronic Numerical Integrator and Computer), the first electronic digital computer, is set up at in Philadelphia, Pennsylvania.

■ *May 4–June 1:* Assault wins the Kentucky Derby, the Preakness Stakes, and the Belmont Stakes, making the horse the winner of the Triple Crown.

■ *July 1:* The United States conducts atomic bomb tests in the Pacific region, at Bikini Atoll.

■ *July 6:* Pauline Betz wins the women's singles title at Wimbledon. The competition resumes after being suspended during the war.

■ *July 7:* Mother Frances Xavier Cabrini becomes the first American to become a saint.

■ *October 6–15:* The St. Louis Cardinals (NL) defeats the Boston Red Sox (AL) to win the World Series.

1947

■ More than 1 million former servicemen enter U.S. colleges under the G.I. Bill of Rights.

■ Women's fashion is dominated by the New Look, created by French designer Christian Dior. It features long, sweeping skirts and cinched waists.

- Jackie Robinson signs with the Brooklyn Dodgers and become the first African American to play in the major leagues.

- Notable novels include *The Big Sky* by A. B. Guthrie, *Gentleman's Agreement* by Laura Z. Hobson, *Under the Volcano* by Malcolm Lowry, *Tales of the South Pacific* by James Michener, and *I, the Jury* by Mickey Spillane.

- *April 7:* The first annual Tony Awards for theater are presented. The award refers to Antoinette Perry, who was director of the American Theater Wing during the war.

- *June 5:* Secretary of State George Marshall proposes the Marshall Plan for the reconstruction of Europe.

- *June 17:* Pan-American Airways begins service around the globe. The first flight is from New York to Newfoundland.

- *June 23:* The anti-labor Taft-Hartley Act passes despite President Truman's veto. The act erases rights granted to unions in the National Labor Relations Act of 1935.

- *September 30–October 6:* The New York Yankees (AL) defeat the Brooklyn Dodgers (NL) to win the World Series.

- *December 5:* Joe Louis defeats Jersey Joe Walcott to win the world heavyweight boxing championship.

- *December 28:* The Chicago Cardinals defeat the Philadelphia Eagles to win the NFL championship, 28 to 21.

1948

- Soviet forces blockade Berlin, which lies in Soviet-controlled East Germany, but U.S. airplanes deliver supplies to the city via the Berlin Airlift.

- Notable novels include *The Naked and the Dead* by Norman Mailer and *The Young Lions* by Irwin Shaw.

- *March 8:* The Supreme Court rules that religious education in public schools violates the First Amendment.

In 1947, Jackie Robinson became the first African American to play Major League Baseball since the sport was segregated in the late 1800s. He was signed by the Brooklyn Dodgers. Manager Branch Rickey told Robinson that as a symbol he would need to be above reproach: "I want a ballplayer with guts enough not to fight back," he said.

"The buck stops here."

—Sign on desk of Harry S Truman

"Me? Naw—I'm prewar," proclaims a youngster in this 1948 cartoon by Bill Mauldin— a comment on the increase in the U.S. birthrate during and after World War II. (*Library of Congress*)

"The most popular, and probably the best, service that Truman could render to his party now is to step aside."

—Newspaper editorial, 1948

▪ *April 3:* President Truman signs the Foreign Assistance Act of 1948. Known as the Marshall Plan, it sets aside more than $5 billion for European reconstruction.

▪ *May 1–June 12:* Citation wins the Kentucky Derby, the Preakness Stakes, and the Belmont Stakes and is awarded the Triple Crown of horseracing.

▪ *June 12:* Ben Hogan wins the U.S. Open golf tournament.

▪ *June 24:* President Truman signs the Selective Service Act.

▪ *July 15:* President Truman and Alben W. Barkley of Kentucky are nominated for president and vice president at the Democratic National Convention.

▪ *July 26:* President Truman signs Executive Order 9981, desegregating the armed forces.

▪ *July 29–August 14:* The United States wins 33 gold medals at the Summer Olympics in London.

▪ *October 6–11:* The Cleveland Indians (AL) defeat the Boston Braves (NL) to win the World Series.

▪ *October 24:* Statesman Bernard Baruch introduces the term *cold war* to describe political relations between communist and noncommunist countries.

▪ *November 2:* Harry Truman and Alben Barkley are elected president and vice president. The electoral vote is 304-189. He defeats Republican Thomas Dewey.

▪ *December 15:* Alger Hiss, former State Department official, is indicted by a federal grand jury on two counts of perjury.

▪ *December 19:* The Philadelphia Eagles defeat the Chicago Cardinals to win the NFL championship, 7 to 0.

1949

▪ The United States has a record national debt of $250 billion.

- President Harry Truman presents to Congress a domestic program called the Fair Deal.

- Notable novels include *The Man with the Golden Arm* by Nelson Algren and *A Rage to Live* by John O'Hara. Nonfiction includes *The Waters of Siloe* by Thomas Merton, *A Guide to Confident Living* by Norman Vincent Peale, and *Peace of Soul* by Fulton J. Sheen. Plays include *Death of a Salesman* by Arthur Miller.

- *April 4:* The North Atlantic Treaty is signed by representatives of several countries, thus creating the North Atlantic Treaty Organization (NATO).

- *April. 20:* The hormone cortisone is discovered.

- *May 31:* The perjury trial of State Department official Alger Hiss begins in New York City.

- *June 22:* Ezzard Charles defeats Jersey Joe Walcott to gain the world heavyweight championship.

- *June 29:* U.S. forces in Korea are removed from the southern part of the peninsula.

- *July 8:* The jury in the Alger Hiss perjury trial is deadlocked. The case is dismissed.

- *October 5–9:* The New York Yankees (AL) defeats the Brooklyn Dodgers (NL) to win the World Series.

- *October 14:* Eleven U.S. communists are convicted of conspiring to advocate the overthrow of the government.

- *November 17:* A new trial of Alger Hiss for perjury opens.

- *December 18:* The Philadelphia Eagles defeat the Los Angeles Rams to win the NFL championship, 14 to 0.

"So attention must be paid. He's not to be allowed to fall into his grave like an old dog."

—Arthur Miller, *Death of a Salesman,* 1949

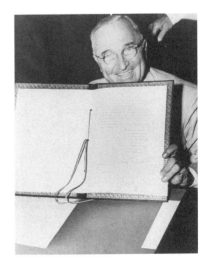

President Harry Truman displays a copy of the North Atlantic Treaty Organization (NATO) Charter, signed by the United States and 11 other countries in Washington, D.C., in April 1949. *(Library of Congress)*

CHAPTER 6

1950–1959

I N 1950, THE U.S. MILITARY ENGAGED WITH COMMUNIST NORTH KOREA, WHICH was encroaching on South Korea. After the conflict ended in 1952, the United States turned inward again, focusing on economic growth and a richer consumer life, made possible in part by mass advertising brought by television. The United States elected its first Republican in decades, Dwight David Eisenhower, former commander of Allied forces in World War II. Yet there were significant undercurrents of social change. The civil rights movement was invigorated by the 1954 decision banning public school segregation, *Brown v. Board of Education.* Implementing the ruling in schools, particularly in the South, brought resistance and violence from segregationists. But public civil rights protests grew, notably in lunch counter sit-ins and the refusal of Rosa Parks to give her bus seat to a white person. Meanwhile, American teenagers set trends in fashion, language, and the rock 'n' roll music that broke onto the scene in 1955 with Bill Haley and later with swivel-hipped Elvis Presley in 1956. One year later, the 1957 Russian launching of *Sputnik* fueled the cold war through the space race of the 1960s.

1950

"I believe that man will not merely endure; he will prevail."

—William Faulkner, in his speech accepting Nobel Prize, 1950

- The population of the United States is 150,697,361, according to the Census.

- Notable novels include *The Wall* by John Hersey, *The Cardinal* by Henry Morton Robinson, and *World Enough and Time* by Robert Penn Warren; nonfiction includes the mental health guide *Dianetics* by L. Ron Hubbard.

- *January 21:* Alger Hiss is convicted on two counts of perjury. He receives two concurrent five-year sentences.

- *April 8–23:* The Minneapolis Lakers defeat the Syracuse Nationals four games to two to win the first National Basketball Association (NBA) championship.

- *June 25:* North Korea launches attacks beyond the 38th parallel into South Korea, beginning the Korean War.

- *July 1:* The first U.S. ground forces arrive in Korea.

- *July 8:* General Douglas MacArthur is named commander of UN forces in Korea.

- *August 4:* The U.S. Army calls up more than 60,000 enlisted reservists for active duty.

- *September 22:* Ralph Bunche wins the Nobel Peace Prize for his work at the United Nations.

- *October 4–7:* The New York Yankees (AL) defeat the Philadelphia Phillies (NL) to win the World Series.

- *October 7:* U.S. troops invade North Korea.

1951

- Notable novels include *Catcher in the Rye* by J. D. Salinger, *Lie Down in Darkness* by William Styron, and *The Caine Mutiny* by Herman Wouk; nonfiction includes *The Sea Around Us* by Rachel Carson.

- *February 26:* The Twenty-second Amendment to the Constitution is adopted, concerning presidential terms. It allows a person to be elected to no more than two terms of the presidency.

- *April 11:* President Harry Truman removes General Douglas MacArthur from command for insubordination.

- *October 4–10:* The New York Yankees (AL) defeat the New York Giants (NL) to win the World Series, four games to two

1952

- The government deficit is $4 billion.

- Employment numbers reach a record high: 62,500,000.

- Notable novels include *Invisible Man* by Ralph Ellison, *The Old Man and the Sea* by Ernest Hemingway, and *East of Eden* by John Steinbeck.

Alger Hiss served as a law clerk on the U.S. Supreme Court and rose to high rank in the State Department before his conviction for perjury in 1950. He served three years of a five-year prison sentence. *(Library of Congress)*

Popular cartoon characters Snoopy and Charlie Brown first appeared in newspapers on October 2, 1950.

"I'd just be the catcher in the rye and all. I know it's crazy."

—J. D. (Jerome David) Salinger, *The Catcher in the Rye,* 1951

Dwight Eisenhower (second from right) and Richard Nixon and their wives, Patricia Ryan Nixon and Mamie Doud Eisenhower, celebrate at the Republican Convention in Philadelphia. The 1952 conventions were the first to be broadcast on national television. *(AP/Wide World)*

"Whoever wants to know the heart and mind of America had better learn baseball."

—Jacques Barzun, *God's Country and Mine,* 1954

■ *February 15–25:* The United States wins four gold medals at the Winter Olympics in Oslo, Norway.

■ *July 16:* President Harry Truman signs the G.I. Bill of Rights for Korean War veterans.

■ *July 19–August 3:* The United States wins 40 gold medals at the Summer Olympics in Helsinki, Finland.

■ *September 23:* Rocky Marciano knocks out Jersey Joe Walcott to win the world heavyweight boxing championship.

■ *October 1–7:* The New York Yankees (AL) defeat the Brooklyn Dodgers (NL) to win the World series.

■ *November 4:* Republican Dwight D. Eisenhower defeats Democrat Adlai Stevenson and is elected president. Richard M. Nixon is vice president.

■ *November 29:* President-elect Eisenhower inspects UN forces in Korea, fulfilling his campaign promise.

■ *December 28:* The Detroit Lions defeat the Cleveland Browns to win the NFL championship, 17 to 7.

1953

■ American deaths in the Korean War total 25,604.

■ U.S. population is more than 160 million.

■ Notable novels include *Go Tell It on the Mountain* by James Baldwin, *The Adventures of Augie March* by Saul Bellow, and *The Bridges at Toko-ri* by James Michener.

■ *January 2:* A Senate subcommittee reports that some of Wisconsin senator Joseph McCarthy's pronouncements of communist infiltration have been fueled by "self-interest."

- *April 4–10:* The Minneapolis Lakers defeat the New York Knickerbockers to win the NBA basketball championship.

- *June 19:* Julius and Ethel Rosenberg are executed for espionage. They were convicted of passing secret information about the atomic bomb to the Soviets.

- *July 27:* The United Nations, North Korean, and Chinese representatives sign the Korean armistice.

- *August 7:* President Eisenhower signs the Refugee Relief Act, allowing over 200,000 refugees to enter the United States.

- *September 30–October 5:* The New York Yankees (AL) defeat the Brooklyn Dodgers (NL) to win the World Series.

- *December 16:* Air Force Major Charles "Chuck" Yeager sets a new airplane speed record, flying a rocket-powered Bell X-1A plane at speeds above 1600 mph.

1954

- President Eisenhower announces that his foreign policy is centered on fighting communism.

- The AFL and CIO labor unions agree to merge.

- About 60 percent of American men smoke; about 30 percent of women do.

- Notable novels include *No Time for Sergeants* by Mac Hyman, and *The Bad Seed* by William March; poetry includes *The Collected Poems of Wallace Stevens.*

- *February 23:* Dr. Jonas Salk begins inoculation of schoolchildren in Pittsburgh, Pennsylvania, against poliomyelitis. Salk is the developer of the serum.

- *March 10:* Duquesne Power Co. in Pittsburgh, Pennsylvania, announces plans for the first atomic power plant

- *April 23–June 17:* The Senate Permanent Subcommittee on Investigations conducts the Army-McCarthy hearings, led

Separated by a wire barrier, Julius and Ethel Rosenberg leave the federal courthouse in New York City after their conviction for spying. Many people in the United States and around the world protested their execution. *(Library of Congress)*

T**he words *under God* were added to the Pledge of Allegiance in June 1954.**

"Have you no sense of decency, sir? At long last, have you no sense of decency?"

—Lawyer Joseph Welch to Senator Joseph McCarthy during the Army-McCarthy hearings, 1954

Bus travel was segregated in the southern states, with separate seating on the bus, separate bathroom facilities and water fountains, and even separate waiting rooms. *(AP/Wide World)*

Actor Fess Parker in costume as Davy Crockett, billed as "King of the Wild Frontier" on his TV show. The price of raccoon skins rose from 2 cents to $5.00 dollars apiece as kids clamored for a cap like the one their hero wore. *(Library of Congress)*

by Republican Senator Joseph McCarthy of Wisconsin, on uncovering communists in the military.

■ *May 17:* The Supreme Court rules in the case of *Brown v. Board of Education* of Topeka, Kansas, and other state cases that segregation according to race is unconstitutional. The ruling prohibits "separate but equal" facilities in public schools.

■ *July 30:* A senator introduces a resolution of censure on Senator Joseph McCarthy for conduct unbecoming a senator.

■ *September 29–October 2:* The New York Giants (NL) defeat the Cleveland Indians (AL) to win the World Series.

■ *September 30:* The USS *Nautilus,* the first atomic-powered submarine, is commissioned in Groton, Connecticut.

■ *December 2:* The Senate, in special session, condemns Senator Joseph McCarthy for his actions in the Senate.

■ *December 26:* The Cleveland Browns defeat the Detroit Lions to win the NFL championship, 56 to 10.

■ *December 31:* Prices on the New York Stock Exchange are the highest since 1929.

1955

■ The U.S. economy enjoys almost full employment.

■ The Museum of Modern Art in New York presents an exhibit of modern American painters such as Willem de Kooning, Robert Motherwell, and Jackson Pollock that establishes American art as a revolutionary force.

■ The Davy Crockett coonskin cap, based on one worn by a children's television character, is highly popular among schoolchildren.

THURGOOD MARSHALL

Born in Baltimore, Maryland, in 1908, Thurgood Marshall began working for the NAACP in 1934 after studying law at Howard University. Armed with a mastery of legal detail and an in-depth knowledge of the Constitution, Marshall won the nickname "Mr. Civil Rights" for his work in many pioneering legal cases in the 1930s and 1940s. Although *Brown v. Board of Education* was his best known Supreme Court case, Marshall argued 32 cases before the Court, winning all but three of them. In 1961, Marshall moved to the judge's bench when President John F. Kennedy appointed him to the U.S. Court of Appeals. Six years later, President Lyndon Johnson named Marshall the first African-American justice on the Supreme Court. Marshall served on the court until retiring in 1991. He died in 1993.

"We conclude that in the field of public education, the doctrine of 'separate but equal' has no place."

—Statement from the U.S. Supreme Court decision, *Brown v. Board of Education,* May 17, 1954

Thurgood Marshall (center) and his fellow NAACP lawyers George E. C. Hayes (left) and James Nabrit Jr. (right), on the steps of the Supreme Court in Washington, D.C., after their victory in *Brown v. Board of Education. (Library of Congress)*

The *Brown v. Board of Education* case was originally brought by Oliver Brown of Topeka, Kansas. He was angry that his daughter Linda had to take a long, dangerous walk across a railyard to a black school when a white school was much closer.

"I had felt for a long time, that if I was ever told to get up so a white person could sit, that I would refuse to do so."

—Rosa Parks, recalling her reasoning for staying seated on an Alabama bus, December 1, 1955

The so-called Big Three carmakers—Chrysler, Ford, and General Motors—dominated the U.S. auto industry in the 1950s. By the end of the decade, many of the smaller independent carmakers—such as Kaiser-Frazer, manufacturers of the models shown in this 1950 ad—had gone out of business. *(Private Collection)*

■ One billion comic books are sold in the United States.

■ Notable novels include *Andersonville* by MacKinlay Kantor, *The Man in the Gray Flannel Suit* by Sloan Wilson and *Marjorie Morningstar* by Herman Wouk; stories include *A Good Man Is Hard to Find and Other Stories* by Flannery O'Connor.

■ *January 19:* The presidential press conference is filmed for television and movies for the first time.

■ *May 23:* The Presbyterian Church approves the ordination of women.

■ *September 8:* A treaty to create the Southeast Asia Treaty Organization (SEATO) is signed by representatives of the United States and several countries in Manila, Philippines.

■ *September 30:* Rising movie star James Dean dies in an automobile accident.

■ *September 21:* Rocky Marciano defeats Archie Moore to retain the world heavyweight boxing championship.

■ *September 26:* The New York Stock Exchange has its biggest one-day dollar loss to date: $14 billion.

■ *September 28–October 4:* The Brooklyn Dodgers (NL) defeat the New York Yankees (AL) to win the World Series.

■ *December 5:* The AFL and CIO formally merge.

■ *December 26:* The Cleveland Browns defeat the Los Angeles Rams to win the NFL championship.

1956

■ The federal minimum wage is raised to $1.00 per hour.

■ Boxer Rocky Marciano retires undefeated as the world heavyweight champion.

- Notable novels include *Peyton Place* by Grace Metalious and *The Last Hurrah* by Edwin O'Connor; collections include *Seize the Day* by Saul Bellow.

- *January 26–February 5:* The United States wins two gold medals for figure skating at the Winter Olympics at Cortina d'Ampezzo, Italy.

- *February 6–8:* Autherine Lucy, the first African-American student at the University of Alabama is suspended, inciting three days of violence on campus.

- *April 19:* Movie star Grace Kelly marries Prince Rainier III of Monaco.

- *July 7:* Shirley Fry wins the women's singles competition at Wimbledon. African-American tennis player Althea Gibson competes and wins in doubles competition.

- *August 11:* Abstract expressionist artist Jackson Pollock dies in an automobile accident at age 44.

- *October 3–10:* The New York Yankees (AL) defeat the Brooklyn Dodgers (NL) to win the World Series.

- *October 8:* New York Yankee pitcher Don Larsen pitches the first no-hit, no-run game ever in World Series competition. The score is 2 to 0.

- *November 6:* Dwight Eisenhower and Richard Nixon are reelected president and vice president. The electoral college vote is 457 to 74. In Congressional elections, Democrats maintain a majority. House Democrats gain a seat, increasing the majority.

- *November 13:* The Supreme Court rules that segregation on buses and streetcars is unconstitutional.

- *November 22–December 8:* The United States wins 32 gold medals at the Summer Olympics in Melbourne, Australia.

- *December 30:* The New York Giants defeat the Chicago Bears to win the NFL championship, 47 to 7.

High-rise apartment buildings like the ones shown here were typical of the kind of public housing constructed during the urban-renewal campaigns of the 1950s. *(Library of Congress)*

"They are the ones of our middle class who have left home, spiritually as well as physically, to take the vows of organization life..."

—William Hollingsworth Whyte Jr., *The Organization Man,* 1956

"Maybe the Russians will steal all our secrets. Then they'll be two years behind."

—Comedian Mort Sahl after the *Sputnik* launch

On orders from Governor Orval Faubus, Arkansas National Guard troops bar African-American students—soon dubbed the Little Rock Nine in the press—from entering Central High. *(Library of Congress)*

1957

▪ New York becomes a one-baseball team town as the New York Giants (NL) move to San Francisco and the Brooklyn Dodgers leave for Los Angeles.

▪ Notable novels include *A Death in the Family* by James Agee, *The Wapshot Chronicles* by John Cheever, *By Love Possessed* by James Gould Cozzens, *Simple Stakes a Claim* by Langston Hughes, and *On the Road* by Jack Kerouac.

▪ *January 14:* Movie star tough guy Humphrey Bogart dies of lung cancer and other complications. He is 57.

▪ *May 2:* Senator Joseph McCarthy of Wisconsin, who sought out Communism in the United States, dies. He is 48.

▪ *July 6:* Althea Gibson wins the women's singles competition at Wimbledon.

▪ *July 12:* Surgeon General Leroy Burney reports that scientific research studies confirm a link between cigarette smoking and lung cancer.

▪ *July 19:* U.S. runner Dan Bowden is the first to break the four-minute mile, running a mile in 3:58.7.

▪ *September 19:* The first underground atomic explosion is conducted, at Las Vegas, Nevada.

▪ *September 24:* President Eisenhower sends 1,000 U.S. Army paratroopers to Little Rock, Arkansas, to quell violence over the forced desegregation of Central High School.

▪ *September 25:* Nine African-American students who were barred from Central High School are permitted to re-enter.

▪ *October 2–10:* The Milwaukee Braves (NL) defeat the New York Yankees (AL) to win the World Series, four games to three.

- *October 4:* The Soviets launch the first artificial sattelite, *Sputnik.*

- *October 16:* The United States officially launches its first objects into space: The U.S. Air Force releases two aluminum pellets into flight.

- *December 29:* The Detroit Lions defeat the Cleveland Browns to win the NFL championship, 59 to 14.

1958

- An economic recession hits nationwide. At its height, more than 5 million Americans are unemployed.

- More than 45 million U.S. households have television sets.

- Notable novels include *Home From the Hill* by William Humphrey and *Lolita* by Vladimir Nabokov; poetry includes *95 Poems* by e. e. cummings; nonfiction includes *The Affluent Society* by John Kenneth Galbraith.

- *January 31: Explorer I,* the first U.S. satellite, is launched from Cape Canaveral, Florida.

- *March 29–April 12:* The St. Louis Hawks defeat the Boston Celtics to win the NBA championship, four games to two.

- *July 5:* Althea Gibson wins the women's singles championship at Wimbledon.

- *July 7:* President Eisenhower signs the Alaska Statehood bill.

- *August 5:* The *Nautilus* makes the first undersea crossing of the North Pole.

- *September 30:* Governor Orval Faubus of Arkansas defies the Supreme Court ruling on school desegregation by closing four public high schools in Little Rock.

- *October 1–9:* The New York Yankees (AL) defeat the Milwaukee Braves (NL) to win the World Series.

"The only people for me are the mad ones, the ones who are mad to live, mad to talk, mad to be saved..."

—From Jack Kerouac's
On the Road, 1957

The clean-cut Cleaver family of *Leave it to Beaver,* which ran from 1957 to 1963, first on CBS and then on ABC, was typical of the wholesome, small-town version of American life presented by TV in the 1950s. *(Library of Congress)*

"We have beaten you to the moon, but you have beaten us in sausage making."

—Khrushchev, referring to the unmanned Soviet spacecraft that reached the moon in 1959, comments on the hot dog, in Des Moines, Iowa, in 1959

Joan Baez sang in coffeehouses and other student hangouts in Palo Alto, California, and Boston, Massachusetts, before her performance at the 1959 Newport, Rhode Island, Folk Festival won her national attention. *(Library of Congress)*

■ *December 28:* The Baltimore Colts defeat the New York Giants to win the NFL championship, 23 to 17.

1959

■ Notable novels include *Henderson the Rain King* by Saul Bellow, *Breakfast at Tiffany's* by Truman Capote, *Advise and Consent* by Allen Drury, and *Goodbye Columbus* by Philip Roth, a novella and stories.

■ *January 3:* President Eisenhower proclaims Alaska as the 49th state in the union.

■ *January 5:* *New York Herald Tribune* reporter Marie Torre begins a ten-day prison sentence for contempt of court after refusing to reveal a source for one of her newspaper columns.

■ *February 28: Discoverer 1,* the first satellite in the U.S. military research satellite program, is launched from Vandenberg Air Force Base in California.

■ *May 28:* The U.S. Army launches two monkeys into space in a rocket from Cape Canaveral, Florida. The rocket reached a height of 300 miles, and the monkeys were recovered unharmed.

■ *June 8:* The Supreme Court rules that congressional and state investigations of communist subversion are unconstitutional.

■ *June 11:* Postmaster General Arthur Summerfield bans *Lady Chatterly's Lover* by D. H. Lawrence from being sent through the mails, based on what he considers its pornographic content.

■ *June 18:* A federal court rules the school law used to close segregated schools in Arkansas unconstitutional.

■ *July 15:* The United Steelworkers of America begin a strike.

■ *July 23:* Vice President Richard Nixon begins a two-week tour of the Soviet Union and Poland.

THE GUGGENHEIM MUSEUM

In architecture, urban office and apartment buildings of the 1950s were usually built in the International Style, which developed before World War II. Buildings constructed in this style were tall, steel-framed structures with glass walls. They were simple in form with little or no decoration. Chicago's Lake Shore Drive Apartments, completed in 1951 and designed by the German-born architect Ludwig Mies van der Rohe is one famous example of the International Style. Another is New York City's Seagram Building, completed in 1958 by van der Rohe and U.S. architect Philip Johnson. One of the greatest buildings of the 1950s, however, was the work of an architect who had started his career in the 1890s: Frank Lloyd Wright. The building was the Guggenheim Museum in New York City. In his plans for the Guggenheim, Wright broke all the rules of traditional museum design. Instead of displaying art in a series of small galleries, the spiral-shaped Guggenheim places the artworks on the curved walls of the building itself. Visitors start at the top level of the museum and view the artworks by walking down a continuous curved ramp. Construction began in 1956 and the museum opened in 1959, three months after Wright's death at the age of 91.

■ *August 12:* Little Rock, Arkansas, public high schools are reopened and integrated. Police forces restrain anti-integration protesters.

■ *August 19:* *Discoverer 6* is launched from Vandenberg Air Force Base in California. It goes into polar orbit.

■ *August 21:* President Eisenhower signs a proclamation admitting Hawaii as the 50th state in the Union.

■ *September 11:* Congress passes a bill instituting the food stamp program for poor Americans.

■ *September 15–27:* Soviet premier Nikita Khruschev visits the United States, making a speech at the United Nations and visiting Camp David.

■ *October 10:* Pan American World Airways announces the beginning of passenger service to circle the globe.

■ *December 19:* The last Civil War veteran dies at age 117.

■ *December 27:* The Baltimore Colts defeat the New York Giants to win the NFL championship, 31 to 16.

A young married couple is portrayed at home. In 1959, the average age at marriage for American women was 19.
(Library of Congress)

CHAPTER 7

1960–1969

JOHN FITZGERALD KENNEDY WAS ELECTED PRESIDENT IN NOVEMBER 1960. THE young president, only 44 years old, ended a Soviet missile crisis in Cuba in 1962 and also started the Peace Corps in 1963. His assassination on November 22, 1963, in Dallas, Texas, brought national mourning. Under President Lyndon Johnson the Civil Rights Act of 1965 protected and advanced the civil rights and liberties of African Americans. It dovetailed with the civil rights movement, led by Martin Luther King Jr. and Malcolm X. Malcolm X was assassinated in September 1965. Martin Luther King Jr.'s assassination in April 1968 led to nationwide grief and urban violence. Two months later, Democratic presidential candidate Robert Kennedy was assassinated in June. The Vietnam War, which had escalated throughout the decade, provoked increasing antiwar protest among young people. Republican Richard Nixon appealed to established middle class voters and promised to end the Vietnam War. The year 1969 closed with renewed hope: the July 20, 1969, moon landing of Neil Armstrong and the U.S. astronauts.

"There's always the possibility that this madman will do anything."

—Senator (later Vice President) Lyndon Johnson on Soviet premier Khrushchev

1960

■ U.S. population is 179,245,000, according to the Census Bureau.

■ Notable novels include *To Kill a Mockingbird* by Harper Lee.

■ *January 2:* Sixteen-year-old Bobby Fischer of New York wins the U.S. chess championship.

■ *May 5:* Soviet premier Nikita Khruschev announces that the Soviets have shot down a U.S. U-2 spy plane and captured its pilot, Francis Gary Powers.

■ *May 19:* Disc jockey Alan Freed, who coined the term *rock 'n' roll,* is arrested on charges of accepting bribes from record companies, or payola, for playing their releases on the radio.

■ *October 5–13:* The Pittsburgh Pirates (NL) defeat the New York Yankees (AL) to win the World Series.

▪ *November 8:* Democrat John Fitzgerald Kennedy defeats Republican Richard Nixon to become president.

▪ *December 26:* The Philadelphia Eagles defeat the Green Bay Packers to win the NFL championship, 17 to 13.

1961

▪ Notable novels include *Catch-22* by Joseph Heller and *The Agony and the Ecstasy* by Irving Stone; story collections include *Franny & Zooey* by J. D. Salinger; poetry includes *Kaddish and Other Poems* by Allen Ginsburg.

In November 1960, Americans elected John F. Kennedy to the presidency. *(Library of Congress)*

▪ *January 3:* The United States breaks diplomatic relations with Cuba, where a revolution has take place. Fidel Castro is the nation's new leader.

▪ *April 17:* The United States authorizes and trains 1,500 anti-Castro Cuban exiles to invade Cuba. The action, known as the Bay of Pigs invasion, fails.

▪ *May 5:* Navy commander Alan Shepard Jr. is the first American to be sent into space.

▪ *June 3–4:* President Kennedy and Premier Nikita Khruschev of the Soviet Union meet in Vienna.

▪ *July 21:* Virgil "Gus" Grissom is the second man put into space by the United States.

▪ *August 13:* Soviet and East Berlin guards set up barriers around East Berlin and begin constructing the Berlin Wall.

▪ *October 1:* Roger Maris of the New York Yankees becomes the first baseball player to hit 61 home runs in a season.

▪ *October 4–9:* The New York Yankees (AL) defeat the Cincinnati Reds (NL) to win the World Series.

"And so, my fellow Americans, ask not what your country can do for you; ask what you can do for your country."

—President John F. Kennedy, inaugural address, January 20, 1961

"As crude a weapon as the cave man's club, the chemical barrage has been hurled against the fabric of life."

—Rachel Louise Carson,
Silent Spring, 1962

John Glenn (center) returned from his space mission a hero and later served 24 years in the U.S. Senate. He returned to space in 1998 aboard the space shuttle at the age of 77. *(NASA)*

- *October 6:* President Kennedy advises families to build or purchase a shelter to protect them from nuclear fallout.

1962

- The twist becomes a popular dance.

- Notable novels include *Another Country* by James Baldwin, *The Thin Red Line* by James Jones, and *Ship of Fools* by Katherine Anne Porter; nonfiction includes *Silent Spring* by Rachel Carson.

- *February 7:* The U.S. trade ban with Cuba goes into effect.

- *February 8:* The Defense Department announces the creation of a new military operation in South Vietnam.

- *February 10:* U-2 pilot Francis Gary Powers is released by Soviet representatives in exchange for Soviet spy Rudolph Abel.

- *February 20:* John Glenn becomes the first American to orbit Earth.

- *February 26:* The Supreme Court rules that segregated facilities at transportation sites are unconstitutional.

- *May 28:* The New York Stock Exchange has its greatest loss in stock value since October 29, 1929.

- *July 10:* Telstar, the experimental communications satellite built by AT&T and Bell Laboratories, is set into orbit.

- *August 27:* Congress approves the Twenty-Fourth Amendment to the Constitution, prohibiting the poll tax.

- *September 20:* Mississippi governor Ross Barnett denies the application of African-American James Meredith to the University of Mississippi.

■ *September 30:* James Meredith is escorted by U.S. marshals to attend the University of Mississippi. Two deaths from mob violence follow; 3,000 federal soldiers maintain order.

■ *October 4–16:* The New York Yankees (AL) defeat the San Francisco Giants (NL) to win the World Series.

■ *October 22:* President Kennedy speaks to the nation about the Cuban Missile Crisis.

■ *October 28:* Premier Khruschev agrees to withdraw Soviet missiles and halt construction of bases in Cuba; President Kennedy vows the United States will not invade Cuba.

1963

■ Notable novels include *The Group* by Mary McCarthy and *Cat's Cradle* by Kurt Vonnegut Jr.; stories include *Raise High the Roof Beam, Carpenters* and *Seymour: An Introduction* by J. D. Salinger; nonfiction includes *Eichmann in Jeruslem: A Report on the Banality of Evil* by Hannah Arendt and *The American Way of Death* by Jessica Mitford.

■ *January 8–March 4:* The *Mona Lisa,* on loan from the Louvre Museum, is displayed in New York and Washington, D.C.

■ *January 28:* South Carolina, the last state to set up racial desegregation, is integrated.

■ *March–June:* The first pop art exhibition is held at the Guggenheim Museum. It includes works by Andy Warhol and Jasper Johns, among others.

■ *April 12:* Reverend Martin Luther King Jr. is arrested in Birmingham, Alabama, during a desegregation drive.

■ *June 10:* President Kennedy signs a bill requiring equal pay for equal work, regardless of the sex of the worker.

■ *July 21:* Jack Nicklaus wins the PGA golf tournament.

■ *October 2–6:* The Los Angeles Dodgers (NL) defeat the New York Yankees (AL) to win the World Series.

On Christmas Eve in 1962, Cuba released 1,113 prisoners captured in the 1961 Bay of Pigs invasion in return for $50 million in medicine and food from the United States.

Dr. Martin Luther King Jr.'s commitment to nonviolence helped convince many white Americans to support the civil rights movement of the 1960s.
(Library of Congress)

Vice President Johnson is sworn in aboard *Air Force One,* the presidential plane, after President Kennedy's assassination in Dallas. A stunned Jackie Kennedy stands at his side. *(Lyndon Baines Johnson Library and Museum)*

The Beatles's first single, "I Want to Hold Your Hand," sold more than 1 million copies within 10 days of being released in the United States in 1964.

- *November 22:* President John Fitzgerald Kennedy is shot and dies in Dallas, Texas.

- *November 22:* Vice President Lyndon Johnson is sworn in president of the United States at 2:39 P.M.

- *November 22:* Presidential assassination suspect Lee Harvey Oswald is apprehended by Dallas police.

- *November 24:* Jack Ruby shoots and kills Lee Harvey Oswald while Oswald is in police custody.

- *November 25:* President Kennedy is buried at Arlington National Cemetery.

- *November 29:* President Johnson establishes the Warren Commission to investigate the death of President Kennedy.

1964

- Racial violence occurs in cities and towns nationwide, including Brooklyn, New York; Chicago, Illinois; Jacksonville, Florida; Philadelphia, Pennsylvania; and Rochester, New York.

- Notable novels include *Herzog* by Saul Bellow and *Julian* by Gore Vidal; nonfiction includes *A Moveable Feast* by Ernest Hemingway, and *Why We Can't Wait* by Reverend Martin Luther King Jr.

- *February 7:* The singing group the Beatles begins their U.S. tour and appear on the *Ed Sullivan Show.*

- *February 25:* Muhammad Ali defeats Sonny Liston to win the world heavyweight boxing championship.

- *March 14:* Jack Ruby is convicted of murder in the killing of Lee Harvey Oswald. Ruby is sentenced to death.

April 22: The World's Fair of 1964–1965 opens amid bad weather and demonstrations for racial equality.

July 2: President Johnson signs the Civil Rights Act of 1964. The event is televised.

August 4: Three civil rights workers are found slain near Philadelphia, Mississippi: James Chaney, from Mississippi, and Andrew Goodman and Michael Schwerner, from New York.

August 5: U.S. planes bomb North Vietnamese naval craft and installations.

August 30: President Johnson signs the Economic Opportunity Act of 1964. It provides nearly $1 billion for antipoverty, youth, small business, and rural programs and a Job Corps training program.

September 27: The Warren Commission report is released. It states that there was no national or international conspiracy to kill President Kennedy and that Lee Harvey Oswald acted alone.

October 7–15: The St. Louis Cardinals (NL) defeat the New York Yankees (AL) to win the World Series.

November 3: Democratic president Lyndon Baines Johnson is reelected. Senator Hubert Humphrey becomes vice president.

1965

Congress passes the Medicare program, providing for national medical coverage.

The London-inspired mod style of geometric shapes, long hair, and short skirts dominates fashion.

Notable stories include *Going to Meet the Man* by James Baldwin and *Everything that Rises Must Converge* by Flannery O'Connor; nonfiction includes *The Autobiography of Malcolm X,* by Malcom X.

Johnson was so far ahead in the polls during the 1964 election, he did not need to campaign much. Here, he waves to supporters in Cleveland, Ohio. *(Lyndon Baines Johnson Library and Museum)*

"If you're born in America with a black skin, you're born in prison."

—Malcolm X (El-Hajj Malik El-shabazz), interview, June 1964

AMERICAN BANDSTAND POPULARIZES ROCK

In the early 1960s, 20 million U.S. teens raced home from school everyday to watch *American Bandstand* on their televisions. Hosted by announcer Dick Clark, the show played teens' favorite rock 'n' roll songs and introduced them to new ones. The songs were often performed live (with lip-synching) by guest stars, such as Chubby Checker, Frankie Avalon, Fabian, or the Everly Brothers. As the songs played, teen couples performed the latest dance crazes. There were also dance contests, spotlight dances, and ratings of new songs.

The show was sometimes criticized for playing only the music of the most clean-cut rock 'n' roll stars rather than the songs of wilder stars, such as Elvis Presley and Hank Ballard. However, the show set another important standard—it was integrated and showed white and black teenagers together for the first time on a national program. It also offered many African-American singers and musicians their first national exposure. *American Bandstand* switched to a weekly format in 1963, but it continued to be broadcast with its ageless host Dick Clark until 1989.

■ *February 21:* Malcolm X is assassinated by rival Black Muslims at the Audubon Ballroom, New York City.

■ *March 8–9:* More than 3,500 Marines land in South Vietnam, the first U.S. combat forces there.

■ *March 21:* Dr. Martin Luther King Jr. leads more than 3,000 protesters on a civil rights march in Alabama.

■ *March 23: Gemini 3,* the first manned Gemini flight, is launched from Cape Kennedy, Florida.

■ *August 11-16:* Racially motivated riots in Watts, in Los Angeles, occur.

■ *October 6–14:* The Los Angeles Dodgers (NL) defeat the Minnesota Twins (AL) to win the World Series.

■ *October 15–16:* Antiwar demonstrations take place across the country.

■ *December 15: Gemini 6* is launched and makes a successful space rendezvous with *Gemini 7*. Pilots are Captain Walter Schirra and Major Thomas Staffford.

The Gemini space program lasted only 2½ years but included 12 missions. This is the view of *Gemini 7* taken from *Gemini 6* as the craft practiced maneuvers. *(NASA)*

1966

■ In the Vietnam War, there are 5,008 troop deaths and 30,093 injuries.

- By the end of the year, there are nearly 400,000 U.S. troops in Southeast Asia.

- Miniskirts, defined as skirts ending four inches or more above the knee, are popular.

- Mind-altering drugs, called hallucinogens, become popular among young adults and spiritual seekers. LSD, or lysergic acid diethylamide, is sometimes delivered on a sugar cube or blotter paper.

- Broadway openings include the musicals *Cabaret* and *Mame*.

- Notable novels include *Tai-Pan* by James Clavell, *The Fixer* by Bernard Malamud, and *Valley of the Dolls* by Jacqueline Susann; poetry includes *Ariel* by the late Sylvia Plath.

- *March 2:* Secretary of Defense Robert McNamara announces that the U.S. troop force numbers 215,000.

- *May 1:* The United States shells Cambodia for the first time during the war.

- *May 15:* Ten thousand U.S. protesters demonstrate at the White House against the Vietnam War.

- *June 8:* The National and American Football Leagues announce a merger, effective in 1970.

- *June 30:* The Supreme Court rules in *Miranda v. Arizona* that the Fifth Amendment applies to self-incrimination during the police interrogation of a criminal suspect.

- *October 5–9:* The Baltimore Orioles defeat the Los Angeles Dodgers to win the World Series.

1967

- Race riots occur in more than 100 U.S. cities over the summer.

- Boxer Muhammad Ali refuses to be drafted into the military for religious reasons and is stripped of his world heavyweight championship status.

"Space—the final frontier…These are the voyages of the starship Enterprise.*"*

—Gene (Eugene Wesley) Roddenberry, *Star Trek*, 1966–1969

Some African-American leaders had philosophical disagreements during the civil rights movement. Malcolm X spoke for many who grew impatient with nonviolence. (*Library of Congress*)

On January 15, 1967, the American and National Football Leagues celebrated their coming union with an end-of-season championship game. But the first Super Bowl, between the Green Bay Packers and the Kansas City Chiefs, disappointed. Not only was it a 35–10 Packers rout, one-third of the seats went unsold.

Vietnam War protestors march on the Pentagon in October 1967. Many veterans of the war took part in this march. *(Lyndon Baines Johnson Library and Museum)*

- Notable novels include *Rosemary's Baby* by Ira Levin, *The Chosen* by Chaim Potok, and *The Confessions of Nat Turner* by William Styron; nonfiction includes *The Medium Is the Message* by Marshall McLuhan and Quentin Fiore.

- *January 3:* Jack Ruby, alleged killer of alleged presidential assassin Lee Harvey Oswald, dies awaiting trial. He is 55.

- *January 15:* The first annual Super Bowl is held to determine the national football championship. The Green Bay Packers (NFL) defeat the Kansas City Chiefs (AFL), 35 to 10.

- *January 27:* Three astronauts in preparation for the Apollo space mission, Roger Chaffee, Virgil "Gus" Grissom, and Edward White II, die at Cape Kennedy, Florida, during a launching pad fire.

- *April 15:* Between 100,000 and 400,000 protesters stage an antiwar demonstration in New York, marching from Central Park to the United Nations headquarters.

- *June 12:* The Supreme Court rules that state laws forbidding interracial marriage are unconstitutional.

- *June 30:* The United States and 45 other nations sign the GATT (General Agreement on Tariffs and Trade) agreements in Geneva, Switzerland.

- *October 2:* Thurgood Marshall is sworn in as the first African-American member of the Supreme Court.

■ *October 4-12:* The St. Louis Cardinals (NL) defeat the Boston Red Sox (AL) to win the World Series.

■ *November 7:* Carl Stokes is elected the first African-American mayor of a large city, Cleveland, Ohio.

■ *November 20:* The U.S. population is 200,000,000.

■ *December 20:* There are 474,000 troops in Vietnam at year's end.

1968

■ The motion picture industry adopts a voluntary new rating system designed to rate movies according to levels of sex, violence, and adult content.

■ Notable novels include *The First Circle* by Alexander Solzhenitsyn and *Couples* by John Updike; nonfiction includes *The Naked Ape* by Desmond Morris.

■ *January 14:* The Green Bay Packers (NFL) defeat the Oakland Raiders (AFL) to win Super Bowl II, 33 to 14.

■ *April 4:* Reverend Martin Luther King Jr. is assassinated in Memphis, Tenn. He is 39.

■ *April 4–9:* Rioting erupts in several cities across the United States following the assassination of Martin Luther King.

■ *April 11:* President Johnson signs the 1968 Civil Rights Act, which makes housing discrimination illegal.

■ *May 2:* Reverend Ralph Abernathy leads the Poor People's March on Washington, D.C., to protest discrimination.

■ *June 5:* Senator Robert F. Kennedy is shot in Los Angeles at 12:15 P.M., following his speech celebrating victory in the June 4 California Democratic primary. Sirhan Sirhan is arrested for the shooting.

■ *June 6:* Robert Kennedy dies from gunshot wounds.

"The individual serves the industrial system not by supplying it with savings and the resulting capital; he serves it by consuming its products."

—John Kenneth Galbraith, *The New Industrial State,* 1967

"In the future everyone will be famous for fifteen minutes."

—Andy Warhol, catalog of photo exhibition, 1968

In August 1968, Abby Hoffman, Timothy Leary, and Jerry Rubin (left to right) announced their plans to disrupt the Democratic National Convention in Chicago. *(AP/Wide World)*

Offered as a free musical experience across the country from Woodstock, the 1969 Altamont, California, Rolling Stones concert broke into violence when the Hell's Angels (unofficial guards) shot and killed a black fan, possibly for getting too near the stage.

■ *June 8:* James Earl Ray is arrested in London for the murder of Dr. Martin Luther King Jr.

■ *June 23:* The Vietnam War becomes the longest war in U.S. history.

■ *August 8:* Richard Nixon and Governor Spiro Agnew are nominated for president and vice presidential candidates at the Republican National Convention.

■ *August 26–29:* Senators Hubert Humphrey and Edmund Muskie are nominated for president and vice presidential candidates at the Democratic National Convention in Chicago. Violence between protesters and police is widespread.

■ *October 2–10:* The Detroit Tigers (AL) defeat the St. Louis Cardinals (NL) to win the World Series.

■ *October 12–27:* The United States wins 45 gold medals at the Summer Olympics in Mexico City. John Carlos and Tommy Smith win medals, but they are suspended from Olympic competition after raising their fists in a black power salute during the awards ceremony.

■ *November 5:* Republican Richard M. Nixon is elected president of the United States, defeating Democrat Hubert Humphrey and third-party candidate George Wallace.

1969

■ Combat deaths in Vietnam exceed 33,000.

■ Large-scale peace demonstrations are held in Washington, D.C., and across the United States.

■ Bell-bottom trousers are the fashion vogue.

■ Broadway and Off-Broadway hits include the racy *Oh! Calcutta!*

■ Notable novels include *Ada* by Vladimir Nabokov, *The Godfather* by Mario Puzo, *Portnoy's Complaint* by Philip

Roth, and *Slaughterhouse-Five* by Kurt Vonnegut Jr.

■ *January 12:* The New York Jets (AFC) defeat the Baltimore Colts (NFC) to win Super Bowl III, 16 to 7.

■ *July 16:* Manned space flight *Apollo 11* is successfully launched. Astronaut crew is Neil Armstrong, Michael Collins, and Edwin "Buzz" Aldrin, Jr.

■ *July 20:* Armstrong and Aldrin descend to the moon, landing at 4:17 P.M. Armstrong walks on the moon, remarking, "That's one small step for [a] man, one giant leap for mankind."

On July 16, 1969, *Apollo 11* astronauts Neil Armstrong and Buzz Aldrin spent 2½ hours on the lunar surface. They collected rocks, conducted experiments, and left behind an American flag. *(NASA)*

■ *August 15–18:* The Woodstock Music and Art Fair is held near Bethel, New York.

■ *Sept. 24:* Eight protesters active during the Democratic National Convention in Chicago are put on trial for attempting to incite riots. When one protester is dropped from the trial, it becomes known as the trial of the Chicago Seven.

■ *October 11–16:* The New York Mets (NL) defeat the Baltimore Orioles (AL) to win the World Series, four games to none.

■ *November 24:* The United States and the Soviet Union sign a multinational nuclear nonproliferation treaty.

■ *December 2:* The Boeing 747 commercial jet makes its first public flight, from Seattle to New York.

CHAPTER 8

1970–1979

I N 1972, RICHARD NIXON WAS REELECTED IN A LANDSLIDE VICTORY AGAINST Democrat George McGovern. During the 1972 election campaign, so-called burglars, actually Republican party operatives, had entered the Democratic Headquarters at the Watergate Hotel in Washington, D.C., to spy.

A Congressional investigation of the break-in revealed a pattern of presidential corruption and the recommendation that Nixon be impeached. On August 6, 1973, Nixon resigned and was succeeded by vice president Gerald Ford. By 1975, the last American troops left Vietnam, the nation remained troubled by social and economic problems such as inflation and gas shortages. Women's rights issues marked the decade, crystallized in the 1973 Supreme Court decision about abortion, *Roe v. Wade*. On a lighter note, blockbuster movies such as the *The Godfather* and *Star Wars* redefined movie genres. The disco dance craze replaced protest-driven rock and folk. The decade ended ominously, when Iranians stormed the American embassy in Teheran, Iran, taking 90 hostages on November 4, 1979.

Major league pitcher Jim Bouton wrote *Ball Four* about his 1969 season with the Seattle Pilots and Houston Astros.

"It seems like a nightmare but this is real. I've really been shot!"

—Alan Canfora, one of the students wounded at Kent State

1970

- Notable novels include *Mr. Sammler's Planet* by Saul Bellow and *Deliverance* by James Dickey; nonfiction includes *Ball Four* by Jim Bouton, *The Sensuous Woman* by "J", *Zelda* by Nancy Milford, *Sexual Politics* by Kate Millett, and *Everything You Always Wanted to Know About Sex* by Dr. David Reuben.

- *February 18:* The Chicago Seven are acquitted of conspiracy charges related to riots at the 1968 Democratic National Convention.

- *April 1:* President Nixon signs a bill outlawing television and radio advertising for cigarettes.

- *April 29:* Fifty thousand U.S. and South Vietnamese troops invade Cambodia.

- *May 4:* At Kent State University, in Kent, Ohio, 4 students are killed and 9 others are wounded by National Guardsmen during a demonstration of 600 antiwar protestors.

▪ *May 9:* One hundred thousand gather for an antiwar demonstration in Washington, D.C.

▪ *September 18:* Jimi Hendrix dies. The guitarist is 27.

▪ *October 10–15:* The Baltimore Orioles (AL) defeat the Cincinnati Reds (NL) to win the World Series.

▪ *October 13:* Militant activist and communist Angela Davis is apprehended in New York for kidnapping, murder, and conspiracy.

▪ *December 23:* The north tower of the World Trade Center in New York becomes the tallest building in the world to date.

1971

▪ Notable novels include *The Exorcist* by William Peter Blatty, *The Book of Daniel* by E. L. Doctorow, and *Rabbit Redux* by John Updike; nonfiction includes *Bury My Heart at Wounded Knee* by Dee Brown.

▪ *January 17* The Baltimore Colts (AFC) defeat the Dallas Cowboys (NFC) to win Super Bowl V, 16 to 13.

▪ *January 25:* Charles Manson and three others are convicted of the murders of Sharon Tate and six others in 1969.

▪ *February 9:* An earthquake strikes southern California, killing 65 people.

▪ *March 1:* The Capitol in Washington, D.C., is bombed by the radical group, the Weather Underground.

▪ *March 29–31:* Lieutenant William Calley Jr. is convicted of the massacre of South Vietnamese civilians at My Lai. He is sentenced to life imprisonment.

▪ *April 20:* The Supreme Court rules that the use of busing between school districts to end racial segregation is constitutional.

Jimi Hendrix's revolutionary guitar style made him an icon to many young musicians. Many imitated him, but few matched his abilities. *(AP/Wide World)*

18-YEAR OLDS GIVEN THE RIGHT TO VOTE

The Twenty-sixth Amendment to the U.S. Constitution was ratified on July 1, 1971, extending voting rights vote to 18-year-olds. In the year immediately prior, many in the United States had complained that 18-year-olds could be drafted into the military and sent off to die for their country, yet they were not allowed to vote for the politicians who might send them there, as the voting age was 21. President Nixon certified the amendment in a signing ceremony at the White House.

U.S. military forces in remained in Vietnam until 1972. *(Library of Congress)*

May 3: The May Day antiwar protest occurs in Washington, D.C., involving thousands of antiwar demonstrators.

June 13: The Pentagon Papers begin to be published in the *New York Times.*

September 5–15: Americans Stan Smith and Billie Jean King win their respective singles championships at the U.S. Open tennis competition.

September 9-13: A prison riot occurs at the Attica State Correctional Facility, in Attica, New York. Forty three people die, including 28 prisoners.

October 9–17: The Pittsburgh Pirates (NL) defeat the Baltimore Orioles (AL), to win the World Series.

December 26–30: The United States resumes massive air bombing of North Vietnam.

1972

Notable novels include *August 1914* by Alexander Solzhenitsyn, *Jonathan Livingston Seagull* by Richard Bach, and *The Optimist's Daughter* by Eudora Welty; nonfiction includes *The Best and the Brightest* by David Halberstam and *The Boys of Summer* by Roger Kahn.

President Nixon shakes hands with Chinese leader Mao Zedong. *(Richard Nixon Presidential Library)*

January 16: The Dallas Cowboys (NFC) defeat the Miami Dolphins (AFC) to win Super Bowl VI, 24 to 3.

February 21–28: President Nixon makes a historic visit to Communist China.

March 22: The Senate passes the Twenty-seventh Amendment to the Constitution, popularly known as the Equal Rights Amendment (FERA). It moves to the individual states for ratification.

■ *May 22–30:* President Nixon become the first president to visit Moscow.

■ *June 17:* The Democratic Party headquarters at the Watergate Hotel in Washington, D.C., is burglarized by five men, including former CIA agent James McCord, working for the Committee to Reelect the President. The event soon becomes known as the Watergate Affair, or just Watergate.

■ *July 11–September 1:* American Bobby Fischer, of New York, wins the world chess championship, defeating Soviet champion Boris Spassky. The event is held in Reykjavik, Iceland.

■ *August 3:* The Senate passes the Strategic Arms Limitation Treaty (SALT).

■ *August 12:* The last U.S. ground combat forces in Vietnam are withdrawn.

■ *August 26–September 11:* The United States wins 33 gold medals at the Summer Olympics in Munich, West Germany. American swimmer Mark Spitz sets an Olympic record, winning seven gold medals.

■ *August 29:* President Nixon announces that an internal investigation of the Watergate break-in reveals no involvement of the current administration.

■ *September 5:* Two Israeli Olympic coaches are killed at the Olympic village in West Berlin by Arab terrorists. Nine Israeli athletes are taken hostage. The hostages and terrorists are killed at a gunfire exchange at the local airport.

■ *September 15:* Five men originally accused of the burglary at the Watergate Hotel are indicted by a federal grand jury.

■ *October 14–22:* The Oakland Athletics (AL) defeat the Cincinnati Reds (NL) to win the World Series.

■ *November 7:* Republican Richard Nixon is reelected president of the United States, defeating Democratic candidate senator George McGovern.

■ *December 7:* The last Apollo space flight, *Apollo 17,* is launched.

GLORIA STEINEM PUBLISHES *MS.* MAGAZINE

In the early 1970s, Gloria Steinem emerged as a leading figure in the budding women's movement. Her experience in the publishing business, fueled by her political views, convinced her a feminist magazine could be profitable and effective. The first issue of *Ms.* was published in 1972. *Ms.* magazine became an icon in the women's movement, while Gloria Steinem became one of the most recognized American feminists in the world.

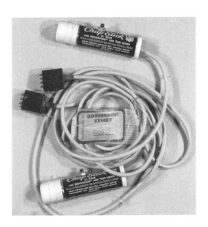

Thin Chapstick tubes compose a so-called bug, which the Watergate burglars planted during their break-in. It functioned as a tiny microphone, so spies could eavesdrop on Democratic campaign plans.
(Library of Congress)

> **T**he Supreme Court decision on January 22 that liberalized abortion laws is known as *Roe v. Wade.*

1973

- Employment rates improve this year but inflation remains high, at 8.5 percent.

- Notable novels include *Gravity's Rainbow* by Thomas Pynchon, *Breakfast of Champions* by Kurt Vonnegut Jr., and *The Onion Field* by Joseph Wambaugh.

- *January 14:* The Miami Dolphins (AFC) defeat the Washington Redskins (NFC) to win Super Bowl VII, 14 to 7.

- *January 22:* The United States, North Vietnam, South Vietnam, and the Vietcong sign a Vietnam peace agreement in Paris.

- *January 22:* The Supreme Court strikes down state laws that restrict or prohibit abortions during the first six months of pregnancy.

- *January 30:* James W. McCord and G. Gordon Liddy are convicted of illegally entering and wiretapping the Democratic Party headquarters in 1972.

- *February 28:* Members of the militant American Indian Movement (AIM) occupy Wounded Knee, South Dakota.

- *May 14: Skylab,* an orbiting space station, is launched.

Unlike the Apollo missions, which consisted of single rockets that left and returned to earth with one team of astronauts, Skylab space station remained in orbit. *(NASA)*

■ *June 16-25:* Soviet secretary Leonid Brezhnev visits the United States.

■ *September 1:* New York State introduces the strictest drug control law in the nation.

■ *September 4:* John Ehrlichmann, G. Gordon Liddy, and two others are indicted for the burglary of Daniel Ellsberg's office.

■ *September 20:* Billie Jean King defeats former tennis champion Bobby Riggs in three sets to win the so-called Battle of the Sexes.

■ *October 10:* Vice President Spiro Agnew resigns and pleads *nolo contendere,* or no contest, to one count of income tax evasion.

■ *October 13–21:* The Oakland Athletics (AL) defeat the New York Mets (NL) to win the World Series.

■ *October 23:* The House of Representatives introduces eight impeachment resolutions against President Nixon.

■ *November 3: Mariner 10* is launched. It is the first attempted U.S. probe of Mercury.

■ *November 21:* The White House reveals an 18½-minute gap in tapes of conversations made there.

> The second of the two World Trade Center towers is completed and opened to the public in 1973. The first tower had been open since 1970, although its upper stories were not finished until 1972.

Gerald Ford impressed senators at his vice-presidential confirmation hearing with his honest, forthright character.
(Ford Presidential Library)

A PRESIDENT RESIGNS

From the discussions I have had with Congressional and other leaders, I have concluded that because of the Watergate matter I might not have the support of the Congress that I would consider necessary to back the very difficult decisions and carry out the duties of this office in the way the interests of the Nation would require.

I have never been a quitter. To leave office before my term is completed is abhorrent to every instinct in my body. But as President, I must put the interest of America first. America needs a full-time President and a full-time Congress, particularly at this time with problems we face at home and abroad.

To continue to fight through the months ahead for my personal vindication would almost totally absorb the time and attention of both the President and the Congress in a period when our entire focus should be on the great issues of peace abroad and prosperity without inflation at home.

Therefore, I shall resign the Presidency effective at noon tomorrow. Vice President Ford will be sworn in as President at that hour in this office.

Farewell. Always give your best. Never get discouraged. Never be petty. Always remember: Others may hate you. Those who hate you don't win unless you hate them. And then you destroy yourself.

—Nixon, farewell speech to the White House staff, August 9, 1974

Richard and Pat Nixon say goodbye to President Gerald and First Lady Betty Ford as the Nixons leave the White House for the last time. *(Nixon Presidential Library)*

▪ *December 10:* Gerald Ford is sworn in as vice president, replacing Vice President Spiro Agnew, who resigned.

▪ *December 15:* The American Psychological Association announces that homosexuality is no longer considered a mental illness.

1974

▪ Inflation during the year reaches 10.3 percent and unemployment hits 7.2 percent.

- Notable books include *Watership Down* by Richard Adams, *If Beale Street Could Talk* by James Baldwin, *Jaws* by Peter Benchley, *Something Happened* by Joseph Heller, *Fear of Flying* by Erica Jong, *Centennial* by James Michener, and *My Life as a Man* by Philip Roth.

- *January 13:* The Miami Dolphins defeat the Minnesota Vikings to win Super Bowl VIII, 24 to 7.

- *February 6:* The House of Representatives approves an impeachment inquiry on President Nixon by the House Judiciary Committee.

- *April 8:* Henry "Hank" Aaron of the Atlanta Braves hits home run 715, becoming more than any other hitter hitter in baseball history.

- *June 12:* Little League baseball announces that its teams are open to girls.

- *August 5:* President Nixon releases transcripts of White House tapes that reveal the president's attempts to block the Watergate investigation.

- *August 8:* In a television address, President Nixon announces that he will resign.

- *August 9:* President Nixon resigns as thirty-seventh president of the United States. Vice President Gerald Ford becomes thirty-eighth president of the United States.

- *September 8:* President Ford pardons President Nixon for any crimes he may have committed while in office.

- *October 12–17:* The Oakland Athletics (AL) defeat the Los Angeles Dodgers (NL) to win the World Series.

- *October 30:* Muhammad Ali defeats George Foreman to recapture the heavyweight boxing championship.

- *November 21:* Congress passes the Freedom of Information Act, over the veto of President Ford.

After assuming the presidency, Gerald Ford appointed the former governor of New York, Nelson Rockefeller, to be his vice president. Nelson Rockefeller was a political moderate and prominent member of a political dynasty founded by his grandfather, the oil baron John D. Rockefeller.

"The chopper had its tail ramp up; I threw in a bag, but I couldn't make it. Someone grabbed my arm and I was dragged onboard and across the floor. Seconds later, in a roar, the chopper lifted off."

—Laurie Palmer, reporter and writer, on the evacuation from Saigon as the North Vietnamese took over the city

1975

▪ The Vietnam War ends. The last Americans leave. North Vietnam increases military efforts in South Vietnam. Cambodia falls to the Khmer Rouge.

▪ Females are now required to have equal access to athletics in public schools and colleges, according to federal guidelines known as Title IX.

▪ Notable novels include *Humboldt's Gift* by Saul Bellow, *Shogun, A Novel of Japan* by James Clavell, *Ragtime* by E. L. Doctorow, *Looking for Mr. Goodbar* by Judith Rossner; non-fiction includes *Against Our Will: Men, Women, and Rape* by Judith Brownmiller.

▪ *January 12:* The Pittsburgh Steelers (AFC) defeat the Minnesota Vikings (NFC) to win Super Bowl IX, 16 to 6.

▪ *April 30:* The final remaining U.S. citizens in Vietnam are airlifted out of the country.

▪ *July 4–5:* Billie Jean King wins the women's singles competition at Wimbledon, Arthur Ashe becomes the first African American to win the men's singles competition.

▪ *July 15:* A joint U.S.-Soviet space venture, the Apollo-Soyuz mission, is begun.

The joint U.S.-Soviet space mission Apollo-Soyuz testified to the huge changes taking place in relations between the superpowers. The scientific cooperation was unprecedented; previously each nation would have been afraid of sharing technological secrets. *(NASA)*

- *September 5:* Lynette "Squeaky" Fromme attempts to assassinate President Ford.

- *September 6–7:* Chris Evert Lloyd wins the women's singles championship at the U.S. Open tennis tournament.

- *October 11–22:* The Cincinnati Reds (NL) defeat the Boston Red Sox (AL) to win the World Series.

- *November 3:* Secretary of state Henry Kissinger resigns as head of the National Security Council. President Ford nominates Donald Rumsfeld for the position.

- *November 10:* A New Jersey Superior Court rules that a respirator attached to comatose woman Karen Anne Quinlan cannot be removed.

1976

- Notable novels include *Roots* by Alex Haley and *Trinity* by Leon Uris.

- *January 18:* The Pittsburgh Steelers (AFC) defeat the Dallas Cowboys (NFC) to win Super Bowl X, 21 to 17.

- *April 22:* Barbara Walters becomes the first woman to anchor a television news program.

- *May 23–June 6:* The Boston Celtics defeat the Phoenix Suns to win the NBA championship, four games to two.

- *May 24:* Concorde supersonic jet service begins between the United States and Europe.

- *July 4:* Various patriotic events are held to celebrate the bicentennial of U.S. independence from the British.

- *July 20:* *Viking I* lands on Mars.

- *October 16–21:* The Cincinnati Reds (NL) defeat the New York Yankees (AL) to win the World Series.

ASSASSINATION ATTEMPTS

Twice in September 1975, President Ford was the target of assassination attempts. Both of these attempts were made by women. During the first attempt, in Sacramento, California, on September 5, Secret Service agents intervened, and subdued the gun-wielding woman, Lynette "Squeaky" Fromme, before shots were fired. On September 22, in San Francisco, the would-be assassin, Sara Jane Moore, fired one shot at Ford but missed by several feet.

Henry Kissinger (above) finally resigned, after a controversial career, in 1975. His replacement, Donald Rumsfeld, went on to a controversial career as well, serving President George Bush nearly 30 years later as secretary of defense. *(Nixon Presidential Library)*

President Jimmy Carter was viewed as a Washington outsider, which appealed to voters disillusioned by the Watergate scandal. *(Library of Congress)*

The Panama Canal Treaties of 1977–78 began the process of handing the canal over to Panamanian control.

▪ *November 2:* Democrat Jimmy Carter is elected president, defeating Republican President Gerald Ford. Walter Mondale is elected vice president.

1977

▪ Notable novels include *Falconer* by John Cheever, *A Book of Common Prayer* by Joan Didion, and *The Thorn Birds* by Colleen McCullough.

▪ *January 9:* The Oakland Raiders (AFL) defeat the Minnesota Vikings (NFL) to win Super Bowl XI, 32 to 14.

▪ *January 21:* President Carter issues a pardon for most Vietnam War draft resisters.

▪ *April 18:* President Carter calls for a nationwide push for energy conservation.

▪ *June 11:* Seattle Slew wins the Belmont Stakes in New York and wins the Triple Crown of horseracing.

▪ *June 19:* Bishop John Neumann, an American, is canonized by the Roman Catholic Church. He is the first American man to be canonized.

▪ *July 28:* The Trans-Alaska pipeline for oil goes into use.

▪ *August 10:* Suspected killer David Berkowitz is arrested in New York. Known as the Son of Sam killer, he is accused of killing six people and wounding seven.

▪ *October 11–18:* The New York Yankees (AL) defeat the Los Angeles Dodgers (NL) to win the World Series.

1978

▪ Inflation rises to eight percent this year.

- Notable novels include *The World According to Garp* by John Irving and *War and Remembrance* by Herman Wouk; stories include *The Stories of John Cheever.*

- *January 9:* A federal judge rules that high school girls cannot be prevented from playing on boys' athletic teams.

- *January 15:* The Dallas Cowboys (NFC) defeat the Denver Broncos (AFC) to win Super Bowl XII, 27 to 10.

- *May 26:* The first legal casino outside of Las Vegas opens in Atlantic City, New Jersey.

- *June 6:* California voters approve Proposition 13, a state initiative to reduce property taxes by more than 50 percent.

- *August 7:* President Carter declares the upstate New York area known as the Love Canal region environmentally unsound and unfit for human habitation.

- *September 6–17:* A Middle East peace conference is held at the presidential retreat at Camp David, Maryland.

- *October 10–17:* The New York Yankees (AL) defeat the Los Angeles Dodgers (NL) to win the World Series.

- *November 18:* In the Central American nation of Guyana, 911 people, many of them Americans, are found dead. Apparently it was a mass suicide by poison, at the People's Temple, a cult led by Jim Jones.

In November 1977, the president of Egypt, Anwar Sadat, made history as the first Arab leader to visit Israel. Israeli president Menachem Begin reciprocated with a visit to Egypt during the following year.

TOGA PARTIES

In 1978, *Newsweek* magazine reported that hundreds of college campuses were holding Roman-style toga parties. In fact, at the University of Wisconsin there was a single toga party with 10,000 attendees. What would cause tens of thousands of young people to wrap themselves in bed sheets and don a wreath on their heads, in the style of the ancient Greeks and Romans? Why, a movie, of course! National Lampoon's *Animal House* was released in 1978. It starred John Belushi, a featured cast member in the immensely popular television show *Saturday Night Live.* In the movie, Belushi and his buddies engage in raucous behavior, including fraternity hazing and campus food fights. In one scene, they dressed themselves in bed sheets and laurel wreaths and the toga party craze was born.

President Carter shakes hands with Anwar Sadat of Egypt (left), after Carter brokered the historic Camp David peace accords between Egypt and Israel. *(Jimmy Carter Presidential Library and Museum)*

- *December 15:* The city of Cleveland, Ohio, defaults on millions of dollars in bank notes.

- *December 15:* The United States and the People's Republic of China agree to open full diplomatic relations in 1979.

1979

- Notable novels include *The Ghost Writer* by Philip Roth and *Sophie's Choice* by William Styron.

- *January 21:* The Pittsburgh Steelers (AFC) defeat the Dallas Cowboys (NFC) to win Super Bowl XIII, 35 to 31.

- *February 8:* As a result of the procommunist Sandanista revolution in Nicaragua, President Carter announces that military ties with Nicaragua are cut. Economic aid is also to be reduced.

- *February 14:* The U.S. ambassador to Afghanistan is kidnapped and killed.

- *March 26:* At the White House, President Anwar el-Sadat of Egypt and Prime Minister Menachem Begin sign an Egyptian-Israeli peace treaty.

- *March 28:* At Three Mile Island nuclear power facility near Harrisburg, Pennsylvania, a power plant malfunctions releasing radiation.

- *October 1–7:* Pope John Paul II visits the United States.

- *October 10–17:* The Pittsburgh Pirates (NL) defeat the Baltimore Orioles (AL) to win the World Series.

- *November 4:* The U.S. embassy in Teheran, Iran, is seized by Islamic revolutionaries. They take 90 hostages, many of them Americans.

CHAPTER 9

1980–1989

I N NOVEMBER 1980, RONALD REAGAN DEFEATED PRESIDENT JIMMY CARTER, promising reduced government and a new conservatism. Reagan oversaw the passage of tax cuts and increased defense spending. He conveyed moral strength and optimism, earning the nickname The Great Communicator, which helped him easily win a second term. Reagan's second administration was affected by the Iran-Contra affair, in which U.S. arms were illegally traded to Iran to get money, which administration officials secretly provided to anticommunist rebels in Nicaragua. Rare diseases, appearing primarily in gay men, led to the discovery of acquired immune deficiency syndrome—or AIDS —soon identified in other victims such as women and blood transfusion recipients. The spread of the personal computer, especially at work and in larger organizations, slowly began to change the everyday lives of Americans and the economy as a whole. For some, young adulthood and money led to greed, as yuppies (young urban professionals) made conspicuous consumption common practice. George Herbert Walker Bush, Reagan's former vice president, was elected president in 1988, promising a "kinder, gentler nation."

1980

■ The population of the United States is 226,504,825, according to the Census.

■ Broadway is marked by revivals, including *The Music Man* and *West Side Story*.

■ Notable novels include *The Covenant* by James Michener, *The Second Coming* by Walker Percy, and *A Confederacy of Dunces* by John Kennedy Toole.

■ The Soviet Union invades the neighboring nation of Afghanistan.

■ *January 4:* President Carter withholds grain shipment to the Soviet Union in protest of the Soviet invasion of Afghanistan.

■ *January 20:* President Carter announces the withdrawal of the U.S. Olympic team from the Summer Olympics in Moscow in protest against the Soviet invasion of Afghanistan.

"While this invasion continues, we and the other nations of the world cannot conduct business as usual with the Soviet Union.... neither the American people nor I will support sending an Olympic team to Moscow."

—President Jimmy Carter, State of the Union address, January 23, 1980

The U.S. hockey team won the gold medal at the 1980 Olympics, defeating the Soviet Union in a thrilling semifinal and then beating Finland in the finals. *(AP/Wide World Photos)*

"In this present crisis, government is not the solution to our problem. Government is the problem."

—Ronald Reagan, inaugural address, 1981

■ *February 12–24:* The United States wins six gold medals at the Winter Olympics at Lake Placid, New York. The U.S. hockey team wins a gold with a surprising win over the Soviet team.

■ *March 17:* President Carter signs the Refugee Act of 1980, which broadens the official definition of refugee and permits 30,000 more refugees to be admitted to the United States each year.

■ *April 24:* A mission to rescue the U.S. hostages in Iran fails. An accident there involving a U.S. helicopter results in eight deaths and five injuries.

■ *May 18:* Mount St. Helens in Washington State erupts in a massive explosion. Fifteen people are killed and thousands of square miles are affected.

■ *October 14–21:* The Philadelphia Phillies (NL) defeat the Kansas City Royals (AL) to win the World Series.

■ *November 4:* Republican Ronald Reagan is elected president, defeating Democratic president Jimmy Carter. The electoral college vote is 489 to 49.

■ *December 8:* Ex-Beatle John Lennon is shot and killed in front of his New York apartment by Mark David Chapman.

1981

■ The nation's population is 230,500,000, according to the census.

■ Notable novels include *The Company of Women* by Mary Gordon, *The Hotel New Hampshire* by John Irving, *Tar Baby* by Toni Morrison, and *Rabbit Is Rich* by John Updike.

■ *January:* Ronald Reagan is inaugurated as president of the United States. At 69, he is the oldest person to become president. George H. W. Bush is vice president.

■ *January 20:* The Iranian hostage crisis ends. Iran releases the 52 U.S. captives held since 1979.

■ *January 25:* The Oakland Raiders (AFL) defeat Philadelphia Eagles (NFL) to win the Super Bowl XV, 27 to 10.

■ *March 30:* President Reagan and his press secretary, James Brady, are shot and wounded in suburban Maryland, near Washington, D.C., by John Hinckley Jr.

■ *July 7:* President Reagan nominates Sandra Day O'Connor to the Supreme Court. She is the first female member of the Supreme Court.

■ *August 3:* Thirteen thousand members of PATCO, the air traffic controllers' union, begin a nationwide strike. President Reagan vows that controllers who do not return to work by August 5 will be fired.

■ *August 5:* Air traffic controllers still on strike are fired.

■ *November 14:* The space shuttle *Columbia* completes its second mission.

■ *December 4:* President Reagan signs an executive order authorizing the use of covert domestic intelligence, the first time in U.S. history that such authorization has been given.

President and Mrs. Reagan attended eight inaugural balls during the evening of January 20, 1981, including one at the Air and Space Museum. *(Ronald Reagan Library)*

1982

■ The Soviet Union intensifies its war with Afghanistan.

■ Unemployment for the year is 9.7 percent. Some 4.6 million people receive unemployment payments, the highest rate since the 1930s.

■ Notable novels include *Oh, What a Paradise It Seems* by John Cheever, *God's Grace* by Bernard Malamud, and *The Mosquito Coast* by Paul Theroux.

■ *January 8:* The American Telephone & Telegraph Company (AT&T) agrees to divest itself of its Bell Telephone operating

"I hope you're all Republicans."

—Ronald Reagan, to doctors at George Washington University Hospital following an assassination attempt

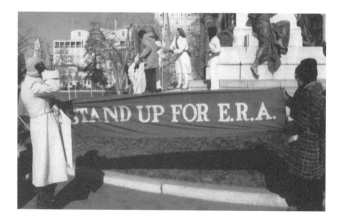

The Equal Rights Amendment remained a controversial topic throughout the 1980s, provoking both support and dissent. These supporters marched in 1980. *(Jimmy Carter Library)*

systems. It had been charged in an antitrust case with monopolizing telephone service in the United States.

▪ *January 24:* The San Francisco 49ers (NFC) defeat the Cincinnati Bengals (AFC) to win Super Bowl XVI, 26 to 21.

▪ *March 10:* The Reagan administration announces sanctions against Libya in response to that nation's association with terrorists.

▪ *June 21:* John Hinckley Jr. is found not guilty by reason of insanity in the trial for shooting President Reagan and staff members.

▪ *June 25:* Alexander Haig resigns as secretary of state. George Schultz is appointed to succeed him.

▪ *June 30:* The Equal Rights Amendment fails to be ratified by the necessary majority of 38 states. Thirty-five states had ratified the amendment since its passage.

▪ *August 20:* About 800 U.S. Marines land in Beirut to help oversee the removal of Palestine Liberation Organization (PLO) forces from Beirut.

▪ *October 12–20:* The St. Louis Cardinals (NL) defeat the Milwaukee Brewers (AL) to win the World Series.

▪ *December 2:* The first successful artificial heart transplant is performed, at Utah Medical Center on a 61-year-old man.

After 2,377 shows, the beloved Broadway musical *Annie* closed on January 2, 1983.

1983

▪ More than 35 million people in the United States live in poverty, according to the Census.

▪ The United States sends military aid to the government of El Salvador to fight its civil war.

- More than 4 million videocassette recorders are sold in the United States.

- The national toy craze is the Cabbage Patch Doll. Some consumers fight over the dolls that are available for sale.

- Notable novels include *Ironweed* by William Kennedy and *The Anatomy Lesson* by Philip Roth; nonfiction includes *In Search of Excellence* by Thomas Peters and Robert Waterman Jr.

- *January 30:* The Washington Redskins (NFC) defeat the Miami Dolphins (AFC) to win Super Bowl XVII, 27 to 17.

- *April 4–9:* The space shuttle *Challenger* makes its first voyage.

- *April 18:* A car bomb strikes the U.S. embassy in Beirut, killing 63 people, 17 of them Americans. The bomb is traced to a pro-Iran group.

- *June 18-24:* The *Challenger* makes its second voyage, this time with the first female astronaut in space, Sally Ride.

- *August 30–September 5:* The third voyage of the *Challenger* has the first African-American astronaut in space, Lieutenant Colonel Guion S. Bluford

- *October 11–16:* The Baltimore Orioles (AL) defeat the Philadelphia Phillies (NL) to win the World Series.

- *October 23:* The U.S. Marine headquarters in Beirut, Lebanon, is destroyed by a truck filled with explosives. The blast kills 241 Marines.

- *October 25:* The United States invades the island of Grenada.

- *November 2:* The Department of Defense reports an end to military actions in Grenada.

- *November 2:* President Reagan signs a bill establishing the third Monday of January, known as Martin Luther King Jr. Day, as an official national holiday.

GAMES AND TOYS

More than 1 million copies of the game Trivial Pursuit were sold in America when it was released in 1983. The next year, 20 million units were sold, reinvigorating the board game industry. Cabbage Patch Dolls were the hot ticket during the 1983 holidays, as people lined up for hours outside toy stores hoping to take home a baby doll for their child. These cuddly, individualized dolls came with a name, birth certificate, and adoption papers. Over 3 million dolls were sold by the end of 1983, with sales of $60 million. The following year, robot figures, particularly Go-Bots and Transformers, were top sellers.

American medical students wait to board a plane for evacuation from Grenada as U.S. servicemen look on. *(DOD Defense Visual Information Center)*

Don Johnson (left) and Phillip Michael Thomas's colorful T-shirts and unstructured jackets worn in the television show *Miami Vice* greatly influenced men's fashion in the mid-1980s. *(Kobal Collection)*

Vice President George H. W. Bush served as acting president for eight hours on July 13, 1985, while Reagan underwent surgery to remove a malignant colon polyp.

1984

▪ The U.S. population is 236, 158,000, according to the Census.

▪ Notable story collections include *Lives of the Poets* by E. L. Doctorow; nonfiction includes *Iacocca* by Lee Iacocca and William Novak.

▪ *January 22:* The Los Angeles Raiders (AFC) defeat the Washington Redskins (NFC) to win Super Bowl XVIII.

▪ *April 26–May 1:* President Reagan visits China.

▪ *August 19:* Lee Trevino wins the PGA golf tournament.

▪ *August 30–September 5:* The space shuttle *Discovery* makes its first voyage.

▪ *September 20:* A car bomb explodes at the U.S. embassy in Beirut, killing 23, two of them Americans.

▪ *October 9–14:* The Detroit Tigers (AL) defeat the San Diego Padres (NL) to win the World Series.

▪ *November 6:* Republicans Ronald Reagan and George Bush are reelected president and vice president.

1985

▪ Despite rising income and lower unemployment, troubling economic signs remain. The national deficit is a record $211,900,000,000.

▪ Notable novels include: *Chapterhouse: Dune* by Frank Herbert, *The Cider House Rules* by John Irving; stories include *The Old Forest and Other Stories* by Peter Taylor; other literature includes *Lake Wobegon Days* by Garrison Keillor.

▪ *April 8:* Following a catastrophic malfunction at a Union Carbide chemical plant in Bhopal, India, that caused 1,700 deaths, the Indian government sues the Union Carbide Corporation.

■ *April 23:* The Coca-Cola Company announces that it is replacing its nearly 100-year-old recipe for the beverage with a new version.

■ *June 14:* Two Shiite Muslims hijack a TWA jetliner in Athens, Greece. Thirty-nine Americans are held hostage.

■ *July 10:* Bowing to the popularity of its old beverage, Coca-Cola Company announces it will reintroduce the former Coca-Cola under the name Classic Coke.

■ *July 13:* President Reagan undergoes surgery for removal of a cancerous colon tumor.

■ *July 19:* New Hampshire high school teacher Christa McAuliffe, 36, is selected as the first civilian to fly aboard the space shuttle.

■ *September 9:* President Reagan announces sanctions against South Africa to protest the country's policy of apartheid.

■ *October 2:* Movie star Rock Hudson dies. He is the first celebrity known to die of AIDS and made his condition public shortly before his death.

■ *October 7–10:* Four members of the Palestine Liberation Front (PLF) hijack the Italian cruise ship *Achille Lauro*. They kill one of the hostages onboard, a wheelchair-bound American Jew, Leon Klinghoffer, whom they throw overboard.

■ *October 19–27:* The Kansas City Royals (AL) defeat the St. Louis Cardinals to win the World Series.

■ *November 20–21:* President Reagan and Secretary Mikhail Gorbachev meet for a summit in Geneva, Switzerland.

■ *December 10:* The American Medical Association recommends a ban on advertising for all tobacco products, citing tobacco's danger to health.

■ *December 12:* President Reagan signs what is known as the Gramm-Rudman bill, aimed at reducing the federal deficit.

In April, the public met a change in Coca-Cola's formula with hostility. The company renamed their old formula Classic Coke and resumed its production.

TERROR AT SEA
On October 7, 1985, terrorists from the Palestine Liberation Front seized the Italian cruise ship *Achille Lauro* as it traveled in the Mediterranean near Egypt. Demanding the release of 50 Palestinian prisoners by Israel, they killed 69-year old American passenger, Leon Klinghoffer, who was confined to a wheelchair, and threw his body overboard.

"Our duty to all human kind is to offer it a safe prospect of peace, a prospect of entering the third millennium without fear."

—General Secretary Mikhail Gorbachev, January 1, 1986, during a televised address to the United States

Associate Justice William Rehnquist was appointed chief justice upon the retirement of Warren Burger. *(Library of Congress)*

▪ *December 27:* Terrorist attacks in Rome and Vienna cause 18 deaths and 110 wounded.

1986

▪ Compact disc sales rise to nearly $1 billion; sales of vinyl records decline.

▪ Notable novels include *The Beet Queen* by Louise Erdrich, *Kate Vaiden* by Reynolds Price, and *A Summons to Memphis* by Peter Taylor; nonfiction includes *Fatherhood* by Bill Cosby and *The Man Who Mistook His Wife for a Hat* by Oliver Sacks.

▪ *January 26:* The Chicago Bears (NFC) defeat the New England Patriots (AFC) to win Super Bowl XX, 46 to 10.

▪ *January 28:* The space shuttle *Challenger* explodes 74 seconds after lifting off from Cape Canaveral, Florida. All seven astronauts aboard, including teacher Christa McAuliffe, die.

▪ *February 26:* Robert Penn Warren becomes the first U.S. poet laureate.

▪ *April 16:* The first surrogate test-tube baby is born, a girl, in Cleveland, Ohio.

▪ *May 25:* Nearly 6 million people link hands from New York to California to raise money for the homeless, part of an action called Hands Across America.

▪ *June:* The U.S. government reports 21,915 cases of AIDS in the country; of that number, 12,008 of those infected have died.

▪ *June 11:* The Supreme Court reaffirms the constitutional right to an abortion.

▪ *June 17:* President Reagan announces that Supreme Court Chief Justice Warren Burger is to retire; Justice William Rehnquist will become Chief Justice. To replace the spot on the Court, President Reagan appoints U.S. Court of Appeals for District of Columbia judge Antonin Scalia.

- *July 27:* Greg LeMond wins the Tour de France. He is the first American to win the bicycle race.

- *August 13:* Congress appropriates $100 million for aid to the Contras, who are rebels fighting against the communist government of Nicaragua.

- *October 18–27:* The New York Mets (NL) defeat the Boston Red Sox (AL) to win the World Series.

- *October–November:* Several American corporations withdraw from South Africa, including Citibank, International Business Machines, and Eastman Kodak, in protest over apartheid.

- *November 3:* The U.S. secret sale of arms to Iran is revealed in a Lebanese magazine article. Repercussions from the sales escalate in the United States into what will become known as the Iran-Contra Affair.

1987

- Nearly 50 percent of American households—43,260,000—have cable television.

- Notable novels include *Beloved* by Toni Morrison, *Presumed Innocent* by Scott Turow, and *The Bonfire of the Vanities* by Tom Wolfe; nonfiction includes *The Closing of the American Mind* by Allan Bloom.

- *January 25:* The New York Giants (NFC) defeat the Denver Broncos (AFC) to win Super Bowl XXI, 39 to 20.

- *February 26:* The Tower Commission Report on the Iran-Contra Affair faults President Reagan for not trying to cease the sale of arms to Iran in an attempt to release hostages held in Lebanon.

On January 23, 1986, the Rock and Roll Hall of Fame inducted its first honorees, including Chuck Berry, Ray Charles, Fats Domino, James Brown, the Everly Brothers, Jerry Lee Lewis, Buddy Holly, and Elvis Presley.

HAWK missiles like those shown here were some of the illegal arms shipped to Iran as part of a plan to exchange arms for American hostages. *(DOD Defense Visual Information Center)*

"The point is, ladies and gentlemen, that greed—for lack of a better word—is good."

—Michael Douglas as Gordon Gekko in Oliver Stone's film *Wall Street,* 1987

JUST SAY NO TO SMOKING

With Surgeon General C. Everett Koop's support, antismoking groups worked diligently. Smoking was restricted or banned in various areas, including schools, public buildings, restaurants, and corporate offices by 40 states, along with hundreds of cities and towns. A new industry sprung up as smokers spent $100 million on programs, clinics, and medications to help them kick the habit.

U.S. Surgeon General C. Everett Koop (right) embarked on an anti-smoking smoking campaign that found support from antismoking activist Patrick Reynolds (left), grandson of tobacco company founder R. J. Reynolds. *(TobaccoFree.org)*

Compact disc (CD) sales surpassed the sales of vinyl albums for the first time in 1988. *(Michele L. Camardella)*

▪ *May 17:* Iraqi warplanes accidentally fire on the USS *Stark,* killing 37 and damaging the vessel in the Persian Gulf. Iraq apologizes.

▪ *August 1:* Mike Tyson wins the unified heavyweight boxing championship.

▪ *October 1:* An earthquake registering 6.1 on the Richter scale strikes the Los Angeles area, resulting in eight deaths.

▪ *October 17–25:* The Minnesota Twins (AL) defeat the St. Louis Cardinals (NL) to win the World Series.

- *October 19:* The New York Stock Exchange has its worst stock crash in history. The Dow Jones Industrial average falls 508 points, representing a fall of 22.8 percent.

- *October 23:* The Senate rejects the nomination of Robert Bork to the Supreme Court.

- *November 18:* The Congressional committees report on the Iran-Contra Affair finds fault with President Reagan for not knowing about his staff's actions in arranging the sale of arms for hostages.

1988

- Rap music gains widespread appeal. Pioneering artists include Run-D.M.C.

- Notable novels include *The Mysteries of Pittsburgh* by Michael Chabon, *Libra* by Don DeLillo, and *Quinn's Book* by William Kennedy; nonfiction includes *Chaos: Making a New Science* by James Gleick and *A Brief History of Time* by Stephen Hawking.

- *February 5:* A federal grand jury in Miami indicts General Manuel Noriega of Panama in connection with illegal drug dealings.

- *March 16:* The United States indicts two government figures in the Iran-Contra Affair: John Poindexter and Lieutenant Colonel Oliver North.

- *April 8:* Television evangelist Jimmy Swaggart is removed from his position as a minister in the Assemblies of God church for misconduct.

- *May 13:* Congress and President Reagan approve a $1 billion program of education and treatment of AIDS. One promising treatment is the drug AZT.

- *May 29–June 1:* President Reagan and Secretary Mikhail Gorbachev hold a summit at Moscow.

COMMON GROUND

Jesse Jackson's speech before the 1988 Democratic National Convention was one of his most inspiring.

Common ground: America is not a blanket woven from one thread, one color, one cloth. When I was a child growing up in Greenville, South Carolina, my grandmamma could not afford a blanket, she didn't complain and we did not freeze. Instead she took pieces of old cloth—patches, wool, silk, gabardine, crockersack—only patches, barely good enough to wipe off your shoes with. But they didn't stay that way very long. With sturdy hands and a strong cord, she sewed them together into a quilt, a thing of beauty and power and culture.... Be as wise as my grandmamma. Pull the patches and the pieces together, bound by a common thread. When we form a great quilt of unity and common ground, we'll have the power to bring about health care and housing and jobs and education and hope to our nation.

"Where was George?"

—Delegates at the 1988
Democratic National
Convention questioning where
George H. W. Bush was during
the Iran-Contra Affair
among other issues

More than 1,200 toxic dump
sites were included on the
Superfund list by mid-1989.
Many sites held hundreds of
55-gallon drums, such as those
shown here full of unidentified
chemicals. *(U.S. Fish and Wildlife
Service)*

June 13: A federal jury in New Jersey finds tobacco maker Liggett Co. guilty in the death of a woman who had smoked heavily for several decades. It is the first time a jury has found a tobacco company guilty.

August 10: President Reagan signs a bill allowing for Japanese Americans interned in the United States during World War II to receive compensation.

September 6: The Census reports that the Hispanic population of the United States has grown to 19.4 million people, or 8.1 percent of the population.

October 15: The Los Angeles Dodgers (NL) defeat the Oakland Athletics (AL) to win the World Series.

November 8: Republican George Bush is elected president of the United States, defeating Gov. Michael Dukakis. J. Danforth Quayle is elected vice president. The electoral college vote is 426-111.

1989

January: The San Francisco 49ers beat the Cincinnati Bengals to win Super Bowl XXIII, 20 to 16.

March 24: The tanker *Exxon Valdez* strikes Alaska's Bligh Reef in Prince William Sound, causing a major oil spill.

May 4: Former National Security Council staff member Oliver North is convicted on charges relating to the Iran-Contra Affair.

August 10: President Bush nominates Army General Colin Powell to be chairman of the Joint Chiefs of Staff. He is the first African American to hold the position.

October 17: An earthquake strikes the San Francisco, California, area before a World Series game is to begin there. There are 62 deaths.

October: The Oakland Athletics (AL) defeat the San Francisco Giants (NL) to win the World Series.

CHAPTER 10

1990–1999

THE DECADE OPENED WITH THE FIRST LARGE-SCALE U.S. MILITARY ACTION SINCE the Vietnam War. When Iraq invaded its small, oil rich neighbor Kuwait, its the United States led an international coalition against the invader, and the conflict ended quickly with Iraq's defeat.

In 1991 the world balance of power changed drastically as the Soviet Union collapsed. Throughout Eastern Europe, Soviet-supported dictatorships and Communist regimes were replaced with free-market economies and democracies. In 1992, Democrat and baby boomer William Jefferson Clinton was elected president. Promising leadership neither liberal or conservative, but "different and ... both," he attempted sweeping changes in policy. He was able to end welfare as it had been implemented but could not achieve health care reform. Yet with increased tax revenue from a high-tech economy and budget cuts, President Clinton ended the budget deficit. Easily winning a second term in 1996, President Clinton oversaw the highest sustained economic growth in peacetime, partly fueled by Internet-related businesses. In his second term, President Clinton was involved in a multilayered scandal involving lying to a grand jury about an intimate relationship with former White House intern Monica Lewinsky. The charges led to impeachment hearings in the Republican-controlled Congress, but the impeachment measure did not pass. At the turn of the millennium the nation was divided into opposing cultural and political camps. The United States had prevailed in the 20th century and become a superpower, but its citizens began the 21st century deeply divided.

1990

▪ *July 20:* Supreme Court Justice William Brennan announces his retirement.

▪ *July 26:* President Bush signs the Americans with Disabilities Act, which prohibits discrimination against the disabled.

▪ *August 2:* Iraq invades Kuwait.

▪ *August 7:* U.S. forces under the banner of Operation Desert Shield leave for Saudi Arabia, where they will defend the country from Iraqi forces that entered Kuwait.

In 1990, Lech Walesa was elected president of Poland. He was the leader of the Solidarity labor union, which had been outlawed by the communists.

Though Operation Desert Shield and Operation Desert Storm defeated the Iraqi army in only four days, U.S. military presence continued in Saudi Arabia and Kuwait throughout the 1990s. One of many young Americans serving in Kuwait, Private Daniel McCullough (above) protects an entry point to a U.S. base. *(U.S. Department of Defense)*

"Putting People First: A National Economic Strategy for America"

—Slogan and economic platform, William Clinton and Al Gore, 1992

▪ *September 27:* Judge David Souter is confirmed by the Senate to become a justice of the Supreme Court.

▪ *November 5:* President Bush signs a deficit reduction bill, aimed at cutting the deficit by $500 billion over five years. Reduction techniques include spending cuts and tax increases.

1991

▪ *January 17:* The United States and its allies begin a massive air attack on Iraq, as part of its Persian Gulf war.

▪ *February 24:* The United States and its allies begin a 100-hour rapid ground war in Iraq.

▪ *February 27:* President Bush orders a cease-fire in Iraq. It marks the U.S.-Allied defeat of Iraq in the Persian Gulf War and the liberation of Kuwait, held by Iraq since August 1990.

▪ *March:* The recession, which has lasted over six months, shows signs of easing.

▪ *April 17:* The Dow Jones Industrial Average closes at an historic high of over 3000.

▪ *October 15:* The Senate approves the nomination of Clarence Thomas to the Supreme Court. Thomas is the second African American to serve on the Court, following Justice Thurgood Marshall. Thomas was cleared of allegations of sexual harassment by aide Anita Hill.

1992

▪ *April 29:* Riots in South-Central Los Angeles follow the acquittal on all but one count for four white policemen involved in the beating case of African-American driver Rodney King in Los Angeles. The riots result in 52 deaths and much damage to property.

■ *August 31:* White supremacist Randall Weaver surrenders to FBI agents at his home in Ruby Ridge, Idaho, following an eleven-day siege. During the standoff, Weaver's wife and son, along with a deputy sheriff, die.

■ *November 3:* Democrat William Jefferson Clinton is elected president of the United States. He defeats Republican President George Bush. Senator Albert Gore is elected vice president.

■ *December 9:* A military force, led by the United States but sanctioned by the United Nations, arrives in Somalia.

■ *December 17:* President Clinton, along with the presidents of Mexico and Canada, signs the North American Free Trade Agreement. It establishes a free trade zone.

1993

■ *February 26:* The parking garage beneath the World Trade Center in New York is hit with a bomb. Six people are killed.

■ *February 28:* Four federal agents die in an unsuccessful attempt to overtake the Branch Davidian compound near Waco, Texas.

■ *March 12:* Janet Reno becomes the first female attorney general.

■ *April 19:* The Branch Davidian compound near Waco, Texas, burns down. Seventy cult members die. The fire ends the siege of the compound by federal agents.

■ *May 20:* President Clinton signs a bill to ease voter registration procedures called the "motor-voter" bill. It allows citizens to register to vote while applying for a driver's license.

■ *July 19:* President Clinton presents a "don't ask, don't tell" policy for dealing with homosexuality in the armed forces.

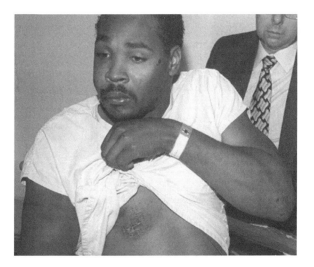

Rodney King shows his injuries in this March 6, 1991, photo. King was beaten by four white Los Angeles police officers after being pulled over for a traffic violation. The videotape of his beating resulted in a federal civil rights trial for the officers. *(AP/Wide World)*

Newly inaugurated Bill Clinton and wife Hillary Clinton share a dance at the inaugural ball January 1993. *(Library of Congress)*

Islamic fundamentalists detonated a bomb on February 26, 1993, in the basement of New York City's World Trade Center. *(NOAA)*

August 10: Judge Ruth Bader Ginsburg is sworn in as justice of the Supreme Court. She is the second woman to hold the position.

November 30: President Clinton signs the gun control measure known as the Brady Bill into law. The law is named for the former press secretary to President Reagan.

1994

January 1: The North American Free Trade Agreement (NAFTA) goes into effect.

January 17: An earthquake strikes Los Angeles, California, resulting in 61 deaths.

February 5: Byron De La Beckwith is convicted of the 1963 murder of civil rights leader Medgar Evers.

March 4: Four men are found guilty in the bombing of the World Trade Center, New York.

August 11: Major League baseball players go on strike.

September 26: President Clinton's health care reform bill is shelved by Senate majority leader George Mitchell.

1995

January 4: As Congress opens, Senator Bob Dole of Kansas is elected Senate majority leader. Rep. Newt Gingrich of Georgia is elected Speaker of the House.

THE OLD MAN WINS

Born in Texas in 1949, boxer George Foreman had many memorable successes in his career. He won the heavyweight championship at the 1968 Olympics, and in 1973 he defeated Joe Frazier to become world heavyweight champion, although he lost that title to Muhammad Ali a year later. In the late 1980s, Foreman was a popular personality, and he became the spokesperson for a best-selling cooking appliance called the George Foreman Grill.

But perhaps his most memorable victory took place in 1994, when, at age 45, he became the oldest fighter ever to win the heavyweight championship, defeating Michael Moorer for the World Boxing Association and International Boxing Federation titles.

- *February 28–March 3:* The Marines aid the United Nations in withdrawing its last peacekeeping troops in Somalia.

- *March 31:* The United States transfers peacekeeping duties in Haiti to the United Nations.

- *April 19:* A truck bomb explodes in Oklahoma City, Oklahoma, killing 168 persons. It is the deadliest terrorist attack in the United States to date.

- *April 21:* Timothy McVeigh is arrested as a suspect in the Oklahoma City bombing.

- *April 25:* The strike of Major League Baseball players ends.

- *June 2:* A U.S. F-16 fighter jet is shot down over Bosnia-Herzegovina

- *June 8:* Scott O'Grady, pilot of the downed fighter jet, is rescued by United states Marines.

- *July 11:* The United States announces that it will reestablish diplomatic relations with Vietnam.

- *October:* The World Series is cancelled, due to the Major League players' strike.

- *October 1:* Ten Muslim militants are convicted in a plot to blow up the UN headquarters and to kill political figures. The plan was not executed.

- *October 3:* Former professional football player O. J. Simpson is found not guilty in the 1994 killing of his ex-wife Nicole Brown Simpson and acquaintance Ronald Goldman.

- *October 16:* Hundreds of thousands of African-American men take part in the Million Man March in Washington, D.C. The march, demonstrating solidarity and steadfastness, is organized by Nation of Islam leader Louis Farrakhan.

> **T**he Dayton Peace Agreement of 1995 kept Bosnia as a single country but split it into two parts, one section dominated by the Muslims and Croats, the other by the Serbs.

O. J. Simpson appears in court, where he tried on one of the leather gloves that prosecutors claimed he wore the night his ex-wife Nicole Brown Simpson and Ron Goldman were murdered. "If it does not fit, you must acquit!" stated his defense lawyer Johnnie Cochran. The saying became a catchphrase during the trial, which lasted five months and was followed closely by the nation. *(AP/Wide World)*

"It was a ball of fire and then the plane traveled down and seemed to break into pieces."

—Debbie Walsh, spectator to crash of TWA flight 800, 1996

In 1996, First Lady Hilary Clinton published a book called *It Takes a Village,* which advocated community participation in helping children develop.

"This is not an industry the American people, I think, can just trust."

—Former Food and Drug Administration Commissioner David Kessler on the health care industry, 1997

■ *November 13:* Five Americans are killed when a military complex is bombed in Riyadh, Saudi Arabia.

■ *November 14–20:* Because Congress and the president face an impasse over budget issues, the federal government shuts down partially. It resumes operation on November 20.

■ *November 21:* Opposing parties in Bosnia and Herzegovina decide to end their warfare. They meet near Dayton, Ohio.

1996

■ *January 26:* The Senate approves the second Strategic Arms Reduction Treaty (START II).

■ *February:* The United States strengthens its embargo on Cuba.

■ *March 18:* John Salvi is convicted of the murder of two receptionists at abortion clinics in Massachusetts in 1994.

■ *June 11:* Senator Robert Dole of Kansas resigns his post as Senate Majority Leader. He is leaving to run for president.

■ *June 12:* Senator Trent Lott of Mississippi is elected Senate Majority Leader.

■ *June 25:* A bomb explodes at a military facility near Dhahran, Saudi Arabia, resulting in the deaths of 19 members of the U.S. military.

■ *July 27:* A bomb explodes in Atlanta, Georgia, near the site of the Olympics. One person is killed.

■ *August 22:* President Clinton signs wide-ranging welfare reform legislation into effect.

■ *September 26:* Twenty-six-year old Shannon Lucid completes an historic 188-day space trip. It is the longest voyage for a female or a U.S. astronaut.

■ *November 5:* Democrat William Clinton is reelected to a second term as president. He defeats Republican Senator Robert Dole of Kansas. Albert Gore is reelected vice president.

1997

- *January 7:* Rep. Newt Gingrich of Georgia is reelected Speaker of the House of Representatives. He is also fined and reprimanded by the House for misuse of donations.

- *January 16:* A bomb is detonated at an abortion clinic in Atlanta, Georgia.

- *January 19:* A bomb is detonated at the Tulsa, Oklahoma, abortion clinic attacked on January 1.

- *January 23:* Madeleine Albright is sworn in as secretary of state, becoming the first woman to hold the position.

- *March 26:* Thirty-nine members of the Heaven's Gate religious cult are found dead in a house in Rancho Santa Fe, California. It appears to be a mass suicide.

- *June 2:* Timothy McVeigh is convicted of murder and conspiracy in the 1995 bombing of the Murrah building in Oklahoma City, Oklahoma.

- *November 12:* Two Islamic terrorists, Ramzi Ahmed Yousef and Eyad Ismoil, are convicted of the 1993 bombing of the World Trade Center in New York City.

- *November 19:* Bobbi McCaughey gives birth to the first set of septuplets who live more than a month.

- *December 23:* Terry Nichols is convicted of charges related to the 1995 Oklahoma City, Oklahoma, bombing.

1998

- *January 21:* Reports say Whitewater independent counsel Kenneth Starr has evidence that President Clinton has had a sexual relationship with intern Monica Lewinsky. President Clinton denies a relationship.

- *January 22:* "Unabomber" Theodore Kaczynski pleads guilty to bombings that killed three people.

Rescue workers move through the wreckage of the Alfred P. Murrah Federal Building in Oklahoma City, Oklahoma, on April 26, 1995. *(FEMA)*

In 1998, consumer prices rose just 1.6 percent. Low inflation was a hallmark of the 1990s, and this was the smallest increase except for one year since 1964.

"I'm king of the world!"

—Director James Cameron, upon receiving Academy Award for *Titanic,* 1998

Monica Lewinsky gained nationwide notoriety for her relationship with President Clinton. *(AP/Wide World)*

"There will be no sanctuary for terrorists. We will defend our people, our interests, and our values."

—President Bill Clinton, on terrorism, 1998

▪ *January 25:* The Denver Broncos defeat the Green Bay Packers to win Super Bowl XXXII, 31 to 24.

▪ *May 14:* Legendary popular singer Frank Sinatra dies; he is 82.

▪ *June 14:* The Chicago Bills defeat the Utah Jazz to win the NBA championship, four games to two.

▪ *August 6:* Monica Lewinsky testifies that she has had a sexual relationship with Bill Clinton but had never been asked to lie about it.

▪ *August 7:* Terrorists bomb U.S. embassies in Kenya and Tanzania, killing 257 people.

▪ *August 17:* In a nationwide address, President Clinton admits an inappropriate relationship with Monica Lewinsky. He also testifies about it to the grand jury.

▪ *August 20:* In response to embassy bombings of August 7, the United States makes strikes in response to terrorist targets in Afghanistan and Sudan.

▪ *September 8:* St. Louis Cardinals hitter Mark McGwire hits his 62nd homerun of the season and surpasses Roger Maris's 1961 record of 61 home runs per season.

▪ *September 9:* Independent counsel Kenneth Starr informs the Senate of evidence he believes may be grounds for impeachment of President Clinton.

▪ *September 13:* Chicago Cubs slugger Sammy Sosa hits home run number 62, tying Mark McGuire's record.

▪ *September 30:* President Clinton announces a budget surplus of $70 billion for the fiscal year 1998. It is the first surplus since 1969.

▪ *October 8:* The House of Representatives votes to recommend that the Clinton impeachment continue.

▪ *October 9–November 7:* The space shuttle *Discovery* is launched and completes its voyage. On board is John Glenn, who was the first astronaut to orbit earth.

■ **November 23:** The four largest tobacco companies in the United States settle lawsuits with 46 states, the District of Columbia, and four territories and agree to pay $206 billion to cover smoking-related public health care costs over the next 25 years.

■ **December 19:** House of Representatives vote for two articles of impeachment on President Clinton. He is charged with one count of perjury to the grand jury and one count of obstruction justice, both in relation to the cover-up of his sexual interaction with Monica Lewinsky.

President Clinton's impeachment inquiry cast a shadow over his achievements. Above he looks thoughtful on his way to the Rose Garden of the White House to make a statement on the inquiry. *(AP/ Wide World)*

1999

■ The Dow Jones Industrial Average closes at a record high: 11,497.12

■ **January 7:** The impeachment trial of President Clinton begins in Washington, D.C.

■ **February 12:** President Clinton is acquitted of impeachment charges.

■ **March 26:** Dr. Jack Kervorkian is convicted of second-degree-murder in the death of one person. Previously, Dr. Kevorkian had assisted over 100 people to effect their own death.

■ **April 20:** Two youths, Dylan Klebold, 17, and Eric Harris, 18, kill twelve fellow students and a teacher at Columbine High School, in Littleton, Colorado. Over thirty people are wounded. The two perpetrators kill themselves.

■ **June 8:** One New York police officer is convicted on an assault charge related to the capture and torture of Abner Louima, a Haitian immigrant.

■ **July 16:** John F. Kennedy Jr. dies in an airplane crash, along with his wife, Carolyn Bessette, and her sister Lauren Bessette.

"There are no good guys in this sordid affair."

—Senator Joseph Biden, on the proceedings surrounding the impeachment of President Clinton, 1999

GLOSSARY

AIDS (acquired immune deficiency syndrome)   A disease that attacks the immune system.

atom bomb (A-bomb, atomic bomb) Highly destructive weapon that gets its force from the release of nuclear energy.

baby boom   The surge in American birth rate between 1946 and 1964. Children born during this period are called baby boomers.

blockade   the setting apart of a country or region by ships or other barriers to prevent trade or communication.

Brown v. Board of Education   The 1954 U.S. Supreme Court decision that struck down public school discrimination in the form of "separate but equal" educational practices.

capitalism   A political system in which individuals, not the state, own and control most of a nation's money and business resources. Goods and money are traded on a free.

civil rights   The freedoms granted a person for being a citizen, such as freedom from discrimination and equal protection under the law.

cold war   A period of distrust between the United States and the Union of Soviet Socialist Republics (Soviet Union), lasting from 1945 to 1991. The mutual tension also affected allies of the two nations.

communism   A political and social system based on government control of finances, resources, and employment.

deficit   A shortfall in a budget, caused by spending more money than is brought in.

depression   A severe, long-lasting economic decline marked by decreased business activity, high unemployment, and falling prices.

fascism   A system of government that centralizes power by means of a dictator, forbidding dissent, setting harsh regulations, or intimidating nation's citizens.

feminism   The social, political, and self-awareness movement for women to gain equal treatment in the workplace and community.

generation gap   Problems in understanding among members of different generations because they have had such varying experiences that they cannot relate to each other.

Great Society   The political program of President Lyndon Johnson. It included civil rights and voting laws and social welfare programs such as Medicare.

imperialism   The practice of a nation extending political authority by acquiring territories or taking political control over nations or regions.

industrialist   A business owner whose company manufactures products, such as automobiles, or controls industries.

inflation   An increase in consumer prices or decreased buying power caused by the increase in amount of money available.

Internet   The worldwide, publicly accessible computer network that consists of multiple computer networks connected to one another.

McCarthyism   The government- and business-supported investigation of American citizens with suspected ties to communism, begun in the late 1940s by Senator Joseph McCarthy of Wisconsin.

millennium   A period of 1,000 years.

New Deal   Political platform and program of President Franklin Delano Roosevelt (1932–1945), marked by a centralized government and more extensive social welfare programs such as Social Security.

New Freedom   Political platform and program of President Woodrow Wilson (1912–1920).

New Frontier   Political platform and program of President John Fitzgerald Kennedy (1961–1963).

Prohibition   The period from 1920 and 1933 that forbade the production, transportation, and consumption of alcoholic beverages. Enacted through the 18th Amendment.

recession   An economic condition marked by higher unemployment and low business and industrial growth.

Roe v. Wade   The 1973 U.S. Supreme Court decision that struck down a Texas law that restricted abortions and effectively made abortion legal.

socialism   A social system in which the making and distribution of goods, and the practice of government is shared by the community.

strike   a work stoppage, usually by a group of laborers that marks disagreement with working conditions or management practices.

suffrage   The right to vote.

union   An official alliance of workers to improve working conditions and wages.

yuppie   Common term for young urban professional; popular name for white-collar working adults in the 1980s.

FURTHER READING

BOOKS

American Social History Project. *Who Built America? Working People and the Nation's Economy, Politics, Culture, and Society, Volume Two: From the Gilded Age to the Present.* New York: Pantheon Books, 1992.

Buhite, Russell D. and David W. Levy, eds. *FDR's Fireside Chats.* New York: Penguin Books, 1993.

Burns, Bree. *America in the 1970s.* Decades of American History. New York: Facts On File, 2006.

Callan, Jim. *America in the 1900s and 1910s.* Decades of American History. New York: Facts On File, 2006.

———. *America in the 1930s.* Decades of American History. New York: Facts On File, 2006.

———. *America in the 1960s.* Decades of American History. New York: Facts On File, 2006.

Camardella, Michele L. *America in the 1980s.* Decades of American History. New York: Facts On File, 2006.

Clinton, Bill. *My Story.* New York: Alfred A. Knopf, 2004.

Cooper, Michael L. *Dust to Eat: Drought and Depression in the 1930s.* New York: Clarion Books, 2004.

Davis, Kenneth C. *Don't Know Much About History: Everything You Need to Know About American History but Never Learned.* New York: Avon Books, 1991.

Gitlin, Todd. *The Sixties: Years of Hope, Days of Rage.* New York: Bantam Books, 1993.

Green, Harvey. *The Uncertainty of Everyday Life 1915–1945.* New York: HarperCollins Publishers, 1992.

Halberstam, David. *The Fifties.* New York: Fawcett Columbine, 1993.

Houle, Michelle M. *Triangle Shirtwaist Factory Fire: Flames of Labor.* Berkeley Heights, N.J.: Enslow Publications, 2002.

House, James and Bradley Steffens. *San Francisco Earthquake.* San Diego, Calif.: Lucent House, 1989.

Jensen, Carl. *Stories That Changed America.* New York: Seven Stories Press, 2000.

Katz, William Loren. *The Great Society to the Reagan Era, 1964–1990.* Austin, Tex.: Raintree Steck-Vaughn, 1993.

Mara, Wil. *Rosa Parks.* New York: Children's Press, 2003.

Meehan, Elizabeth. *Twentieth-Century American Writers.* San Diego, Calif.: Lucent Books, 2000.

Meltzer, Milton. *There Comes a Time: The Struggle for Civil Rights.* New York: Random House, 2001.

Myers, Walter Dean, illustrated by Leonard Jenkins. *I've Seen the Promised Land: The Life of Dr. Martin Luther King, Jr.* New York: HarperCollins, 2004.

O'Neal, Michael J. *America in the 1920s.* Decades of American History. New York: Facts On File, 2006.

Ochoa, George. *America in the 1990s.* Decades of American History. New York: Facts On File, 2006.

Pendergast, Sara and Tom Pendergast, eds. *Bowling, Beatniks, and Bell-bottoms: Pop Culture of 20th Century America, 5 vols.* Detroit, Mich.: UXL, 2002.

Ravitch, Diane, ed. *The American Reader: Words That Moved a Nation.* New York: Harper Perennial, 1991.

Sandler, Martin W., Introduction by James H. Billington. *Inventors*. New York: Harper Collins, 1996.

Schlereth, Thomas J. *Victorian America: Transformations in Everyday Life, 1876–1915*. New York: HarperPerennial, 1992.

Schomp, Virginia. *World War II*. New York: Benchmark Books, 2001.

Strasser, Susan. *Never Done: A History of American Housework*. New York: Pantheon Books, 1982.

The World Almanac Book of Facts 1999. Mahwah, N.J.; World Almanac Books, 1998.

Wills, Charles A. *America in the 1940s*. Decades of American History. New York: Facts On File, 2006.

———. *America in the 1950s*. Decades of American History. New York: Facts On File, 2006.

Zeinert, Karen. *McCarthy and the Fear of Communism in American History*. Springfield, N.J.: Enslow Publications, 1998.

Zinn, Howard. *A People's History of the United States: 1492–Present*. New York: Perennial Classics, 2001.

WEB SITES

Academy of Achievement. "The Achiever Gallery." Available online. URL: http://www.achievement.org. Downloaded in August 2005.

Kingwood College Library. "American Cultural History: The Twentieth Century." Available online. URL: http://kclibrary.nhmccd.edu/decades.html. Updated in July 2001.

Library of Congress. "America's Story from America's Library." Available online. URL: http://www.americaslibrary.gov. Downloaded in August 2005.

———. "American Memory." Available online. URL: http://memory.loc.gov/ammem. Downloaded in August 2005.

Teacher Net. "20th Century American Culture." Available online. URL: http://members.aol.com/TeacherNet/20CC.html. Downloaded in August 2005.

Timeline of American History. Available online. URL: http://history1900s.about.com/library/weekly/aa110900a.htm. Downloaded in August 2005.

U.S. Department of State Bureau of International Information Programs. "An Outline of American History." Available online. URL: http://usinfo.state.gov/products/pubs/history/toc.htm. Posted in March 1999.

Wikipedia, the Free Encyclopedia. "20th-Century History and Profiles of Leaders." Available online. URL: http://en.wikipedia.org/wiki/20th_century. Downloaded in August 2005.

World Almanac for Kids. "American History Timeline." Available online. URL: http://www.worldalmanacforkids.com/explore/timeline4.html. Downloaded in August 2005.

INDEX

Page numbers in *italics* indicate illustrations. Page numbers followed by *g* indicate glossary entries. Page numbers in **boldface** indicate box features.

A

Aaron, Hank 93
Abel, Rudolph 76
abortion 90, 106
Achille Lauro hostages 105
acquired immune deficiency syndrome. *See* AIDS
Addams, Jane 6
Afghanistan invasion 99
African Americans 5, 6, 11, 59, 62, 70, 115. *See also* civil rights
Age of Innocence, The (Wharton) 22
Agnew, Spiro 84, 91, 92
Agony and the Ecstasy, The (Stone) 75
Agricultural Adjustment Act (AAA) 38, 43
AIDS 99, 105, 106, 109, 120*g*
Albright, Madeleine 117
Aldrin, Buzz 85
Alice Adams (Tarkington) 23
All the King's Men (Warren) 58
American Bandstand (television show) **80**
American Federation of Labor (AFL) 23, 37, 39, 42, 65, 68
American Indian Movement (AIM) 90
American Language, The (Mencken) 20
American Psychological Association (APA) 92
American Telephone & Telegraph Company (AT&T) 101–102
American Tragedy, An (Dreiser) 26
Americans with Disabilities Act (1990) 111
Anderson, Marian *48*
Animal House (film) **97**
Apollo space program 82, 85, 89, 90
Ariel (Plath) 81
Armistice Day 23
Armstrong, Neil 74, 85
Army, U.S. 37, 72
assembly line 11, 21
Atlantic Charter 50

atomic bomb 33, *57*, 58, 65, 120*g*
Autobiography of Alice B. Toklas, The (Stein) 37
aviation 5, 7, 29, 34–35, 46, 73

B

Babbitt (Lewis) 24
baby boom, 60, 120*g*
Baez, Joan *72*
Banking Act (1933) 38
Barkley, Alben 60
Barnett, Ross 76
Baruch, Bernard 60
Bataan Death March 52
Baum, L. Frank 5
Bay of Pigs invasion 75, 77
Beatles, The 78
Beautiful and Damned, The (Fitzgerald) 24
Beckwith, Byron De La 114
Begin, Menachem 97, 98
Bell Telephone 101
Bellow, Saul 69, 78, 94
Beloved (Morrison) 107
Berkowitz, David 96
Berlin Wall 75
Bessette, Carolyn 119
Biden, Joseph 119
Billy Budd (Melville) 25
birth control 15, 17
Birth of a Nation, The (film) 16
Black Power 84
Black Tuesday 31
Bluford, Guion S. 103
Bonfire of the Vanities, The (Wolfe) 107
Boy Scouts 12
Brady Bill 114
Brady, James 101
Brandeis, Louis 17
Breakfast at Tiffany's (Capote) 72
Brennan, William 111
Brief History of Time, A (Hawking) 109
Brown v. Board of Education (1954) 62, 66, **67**, 120*g*
Bryan, William Jennings 6, 27
Bunche, Ralph 63
Burger, Warren 106
Burney, Leroy 70
Bush, George H. W. 99, 104, 110–113

C

Cabbages and Kings (O. Henry) 7

Call of the Wild, The (London) 7
Camp David Accords 97, *98*
Capone, Al 23, 31, *33*, 35
Capote, Truman 72
Carnegie, Andrew 6, **15**
Carrier, Willis 6
cars 5, 11, 20, 21, 41, 68
Carter, Jimmy 96–98, 99–100
Casablanca (film) 54
Castro, Fidel 75
Catch-22 (Heller) 75
Catcher in the Rye (Salinger) 63
Cat's Cradle (Vonnegut) 77
Central Intelligence Agency (CIA) 89
Challenger space program 103, 106
Cheever, John 96, 101
China 88, 104
Chosen, The (Potok) 82
Churchill, Winston 50, 55
Cider House Rules, The (Irving) 104
cigarettes 31, 70, 86, 105, 108, 110
Circular Staircase, The (Rinehart) 10
Civil Aeronautics Act 46
civil rights 62, 113, 120*g*
African American 9, 74, 81
Civil Rights Act (1964) 79
Civil Rights Act (1968) 83
Civil Works Administration 37, 39
Civilian Conservation Corps (CCC) 32, 38, 39
Clansman, The (Dixon) 8
Clark, Dick 80
Clavell, James 81
Clayton Antitrust Act (1914) 15
Clinton, Hillary *113*
Clinton, William 111, 112–114, 116–119
Coca-Cola 105
Cochran, Johnnie 115
cold war 60, 62, 120*g*
Collins, Michael 85
Columbine High School (Colorado) 119
Committee to Investigate Un-American Activities (HUAC) 46
Common Sense Book of Baby and Child Care (Spock) 58
communism 19, 24, 64–66, 70, 88, 111, 120*g*

compact discs 106
Confederacy of Dunces, A (Toole) 99
Confessions of an Ex-Colored Man (Johnson) 13
Congress 18
Congress of Industrial Organizations (CIO) 46, 65, 68
conservation 5
Constitution, U.S. 14, 20, 24, 26, 63, **87**
Contras 107
Coolidge, Calvin 21, 22, 24, *28*, 29
Cuba 75, 76, 77, 116
Cuban Missile Crisis 74
Curtis, Charles 30, 31
Czolgosz, Leon 5

D

Davis, Angela 87
Davis, John W. 26
Dawes, Charles 26
de Kooning, Willem 66
Death Comes for the Archbishop (Cather) 28
Death of a Salesman (Miller) 61
Debs, Eugene V. 8
Deliverance (Dickey) 86
DeMille, Cecil B. 14
Democracy and Education (Dewey) 17
Democracy and Social Action (Addams) 6
Devil's Dictionary, The (Bierce) 12
Dewey, John 24
DiMaggio, Joe 50, **53**
Discoverer satellite program 72, 73
Discovery space shuttle 118
Disney, Walt 30
Doctorow, E. L. 87, 94, 104
Dole, Robert 116
Dreiser, Theodore 5, 13, 26
drugs 81
Du Bois, W. E. B. 7, 9, 10
Dukakis, Michael 110
Durant, W. C. 12

E

Earhart, Amelia 30, 36
earthquakes 9, 110
Economic Opportunity Act (1964) 79
economy 14, 33, 46, 60, 111. *See also* Great Depression

Ed Sullivan Show (television show) 78
Egyptian-Israeli prace treaty 98
Ehrlichmann, John 91
Eighteenth Amendment 20
Eisenhower, Dwight D. 55, 62, 64–73
Eisenhower, Maime Doud *64*
El Salvador 102
Electronic Numerical Integrator and Computer (ENIAC) 58
Eliot, T. S. 24
Ellison, Ralph 63
Ellsberg, Daniel 91
Emergency Relief Appropriation Act 41
employment 90. *See also* unemployment
Equal Rights Amendment (ERA) 88, 102
Espionage Act (1917) 17
Ethan Frome (Wharton) 12
Evers, Medgar 114
Exorcist, The (Blatty) 87
Explorer (space satellite) 71
Exxon Valdez oil spill 110

F

Fair Deal 61
Fairbanks, Charles W. 8
Farewell to Arms, A (Hemingway) 31
Farrakhan, Louis 115
fashion 58, 79, 81, 84
Faulkner, William 27, *29*, 31, 32, 34, 45, 48, 62
Federal Bureau of Investigation (FBI) 10
Federal Deposit Insurance Corporation (FDIC) 32, 38
feminism **89**, 120*g. See also* women
Ferdinand, Franz 15
Financier, The (Dreiser) 13
fireside chats 38, *40*, 48
Fitzgerald, F. Scott 22, 24, 26, 39
Food and Drug Administration (FDA) 116
food stamps 73
For Whom the Bell Tolls (Hemingway) 49
Ford, Gerald 86, 91–96
Ford, Henry 5, 6, 7, 11, 18, 21
Four Million, The (O. Henry) 9
Fourteen Points 19
Franny & Zooey (Salinger) 75

Freed, Alan 74
Freedom of Information Act 93
Fromme, Lynette "Squeaky" 95
Frost, Robert 15, 48

G

Galbraith, John Kenneth 83
games **103**
Garner, John Nance 36
Gemini space program 80
General Agreement on Tariffs and Trade (GATT) 82
General Electric 31
General Motors 10, 31
G.I. Bill of Rights 58, 64
Gingrich, Newt 116
Ginsburg, Allen 75
Ginsburg, Ruth Bader 114
Glenn, John 76, 118
Godfather, The (film) 86
Godfather, The (Puzo) 84
Goldman, Ronald 115
Gompers, Samuel 23
Gone With the Wind (film) 32, 43, 47
Good Man is Hard to Find and Other Stories, A (O'Connor) 68
Gorbachev, Mikhail 106, 109
Gore, Al 112
Gramm-Rudman bill 105
Grapes of Wrath, The (Steinbeck) 48
Gravity's Rainbow (Pynchon) 90
Great Depression, 21, 32–36, 120*g*
Great Gatsby, The (Fitzgerald) 26
Great Migration 11
Great Train Robbery, The (film) 7
Great Zigfield, The (film) 43
Griffith, D. W. 16
Grissom, Virgil ("Gus") 75
Guggenheim Museum **73**
Guthrie, A. B. 59

H

Haig, Alexander 102
Haiti 114
Haley, Alex 95
Hands Across America 106
Harding, Warren G. 21, 22, 24, 25
Hardwick, Thomas 24
Hawking, Stephen 109
Heller, Joseph 75, 93

Hemingway, Ernest 27, 31, 37, 45, 63
Henderson the Rain King (Bellow) 72
Hendrix, Jimi 87
Hill, Anita 112
Hinckley, John, Jr. 101, 102
Hindenburg crash 43, 44
Hiss, Alger 60, 61, 62, *63*
History of the Standard Oil Company (Tarbell) 7
Holiday, Billie 73
Homestead Act (1909) 10
homosexuality 92, 113
Hoover, Herbert 21, 30, 31, 33, 35, 36, *38*
House of Mirth, The (Wharton) 8
Hughes, Langston 27
Humphrey, Hubert 79

I

Iacocca, Lee 104
Industrial Workers of the World (IWW) 8, 13. *See also* Wobblies
inflation 90, 92, 96, 120*g*
Informer, The (film) 41
Internet 111, 120*g*
interracial marriage 82
Intolerance (film) 16
Iran-Contra Affair 99, 107, 109, 110
Iran hostage crisis 86, 98, 100, 101
Irving, John 97, 100, 104
Ismoil, Eyad 117
It Happened One Night (film) 39

J

Jackson, Jesse **109**
James, Henry 6, **8**
Japanese Americans 110
Jaws (Benchley) 93
Johns, Jasper 77
Johnson, Jack 10
Johnson, Lyndon Baines 67, 74, 78–79, 83
Jones, Jim 97
Jong, Erica 93
Joyce, James 39
Julian (Vidal) 78
Jungle, The (Sinclair) 8, 9, **10**

K

Kaczynski, Theodore 117
Keillor, Garrison 104

Keller, Helen 6
Kellogg-Briand Pact 30, 31
Kennedy, Jackie *78*
Kennedy, John F., Jr. 119
Kennedy, John Fitzgerald 74–78
Kennedy, Robert F. 74, 83
Kerouac, Jack 70, 71
Kervorkian, Jack 119
Kessler, David 116
Khruschev, Nikita 73, 74, 75, 77
King, Martin Luther, Jr. 74, *77*, 80, 83, 84, 103
King, Rodney 112, *113*
Kissinger, Henry 95
Koop, C. Everett **108**
Korean War 62, 64
Ku Klux Klan (KKK) 15, 16, 23, 27, *28*
Kuwait 111–112

L

Lady Chatterly's Lover (Lawrence) 72
Lawrence, D. H. 72
League of Nations 11, 20, 21
Leave it to Beaver (television show) 71
Lee, Harper 74
Lend Lease Bill (1941) 50
Lennon, John 100
Lewinsky, Monica 111, 117, *118*, 119
Lewis, John L. 42
Lewis, Sinclair 24, 26, 28, 33, 56
Liddy, G. Gordon 90, 91
Lindbergh, Charles 29, 35–36
Little Rock (Arkansas) 70, 71, 73
Lolita (Nabokov) 71
Lomax, Alan **47**
London, Jack 7
Long, Huey 42
Lost Lady, A (Cather) 25
Lott, Trent 116
Louima, Abner 119
Lucid, Shannon 116
Lusitania sinking 16

M

MacArthur, Douglas 36, 52, 57, 62
Mailer, Norman 59
Malcolm X 74, 79, 80, *81*
Man Who Knew Coolidge, The (Lewis) 30
Manson, Charles 87
Mariner (space probe) 91

Maris, Roger 75
Marshall, Thurgood *67*, 82, 112
Martin Eden (London) 10
McCarthy, Joseph 64, 66, 70
McCaughey, Bobbi 117
McCord, James W. 90
McCullough, Daniel 112
McGovern, George 86
McKinley, William 5, 6
McNamara, Robert 81
McVeigh, Timothy 115, 117
Medicare 79
Melville, Herman 25
Meredith, James 76, 77
Miami Vice (television show) 104
millennium 111, 120*g*
Miller, Arthur 61
Million Man March 115
Mind of the Primitive Man, The (Boas) 12
Miranda v. Arizona (1966) 81
Mitchell, George 114
Model T car 5, 14, *18*, 28
Morgan, J. P. 6, **15**
Morgan, Thomas Hunt 39
Morrison, Toni 100, 107
Mother Jones 7
Motherwell, Robert 66
movies. *See* films
Mr. Deeds Goes to Town (film) 43
Mr. Smith Goes to Washington (film) 47
muckraking 5, 9, **10**
music 74, **80**, 107, 109
Muskie, Edmund 84

N

Nabokov, Vladimir 71, 84
Nation of Islam 115
National Association for the Advancement of Colored People (NAACP) 5, 10, *67*
National Industrial Recovery Act (NIR) 38
National Labor Relations Act (1935) 44
National Recovery Act (NRA) 38
National Recovery Administration (NRA) 41
Navy, U.S. 24
Ness, Eliot 23
Neutrality Act (1939) 48
New Deal 32, 120*g*
New York Stock Exchange crash 109
Niagara Movement 9

Nicaragua 27, 98, 99, 107
Nichols, Terry 117
Nineteenth Amendment 24
Nixon, Patricia *64*, *92*
Nixon, Richard *64*, 69, 72, 74, 84, 86–93
Noriega, Manuel 109
Norris, Frank 6
North American Free Trade Agreement (NAFTA) 113, 114
North Atlantic Treaty Organization (NATO) 61
nylon **51**

O

O Pioneers! (Cather) 14
O'Connor, Flannery 68, 79
O'Connor, Sandra Day 101
Octopus, The (Norris) 6
Of Mice and Men (Steinbeck) 44
Office of Price Administration and Cilivial Supply (OPA) 50, 51
O'Grady, Scott 115
Oil! (Sinclair) 28
Oklahoma City bombing 114, 115, 117
Oklahoma! (musical) 53, *54*
On the Road (Kerouac) 70, 71
One of Ours (Cather) 24
Operation Desert Shield 111, 112
Oswald, Lee Harvey 78, 82

P

Palestine Liberation Front (PLF) 105
Palmer, A. Mitchell 19
Pan-American Exposition 6
Panama 109
Panama Canal 5, 7, 15, *16*, 46
Panama Canal Treaties 96
Parker, Alton B. 8
Parks, Rosa 62, 68
payola scandal 74
Peace Corps 74
Pearl Harbor bombing 50
Peary, Robert Edwin 10
Penrod (Tarkington) 15
Persian Gulf war 111–112
Philippines 5, 39, 50, 56, 57
Plath, Sylvia 81
Pledge of Allegiance 65
Poindexter, John 109
Poland 72

polio vaccine 65
poll tax 76
Pollock, Jackson 66
Polyanna (Porter) 14
Porter, Edwin S. 7
Porter, William Sydney (O. Henry) 7
Potok, Chaim 82
poverty 102
Powell, Colin 110
Powers, Francis Gary 74, 76
Pragmatism (James) 9
Presley, Elvis 62, 107
Professional Air Traffic Controllers Organization (PATCO) 101
prohibition 11, 21, 120*g*
Public Works Administration (PWA) 38
Puzo, Mario 84
Pynchon, Thomas 90

Q

Quayle, Dan 110

R

radio 9, 47
Ragtime (Doctorow) 94
rap music 109
rationing 52, 54, 55, 57
Ray, James Earl 84
Reagan, Nancy *101*
Reagan, Ronald 99, 100–107, 109–110, 114
Red Scare 19, 24
Refugee Act (1980) 100
Rehnquist, William 106
Renascence (Millay) 18
Reno, Janet 113
Revenue Bill (1938) 46
Reynolds, R. J. **108**
Ride, Sally 103
riots, race 54, 78, 81
Rising Tide, The (Cabell) 17
Robinson, Jackie 59
Robinson, Joseph T. 30, 31
rock 'n' roll 74, **80**, 107
Rockefeller, John D. **15**, 93
Rockefeller, Nelson 93
Roe v. Wade (1973) 86, 90, 120*g*
Rolling Stones 84
Roosevelt, Eleanor 48
Roosevelt, Franklin Delano 32, 37, 38, 40–56
Roosevelt, Theodore (Teddy) 5–10, 11, 14, 28, 32

Roots (Haley) 95
Rosary, The (Barclay) 11
Rosemary's Baby (Levin) 82
Rosenberg, Ethel *65*
Rosenberg, Julius *65*
Roth, Philip 93
Ruby, Jack 78, 82
Rumsfeld, Donald 95
Russo-Japanese War 9
Ruth, Babe 28

S

Sacco and Vanzetti trial 22, 29
Sadat, Anwar 97, 98
Salinger, J. D. 63, 75, 77
Salk, Jonas 65
Salvi, John 116
San Francisco earthquakes 9, 110
Sandainstas 98
Sanger, Margaret 15
Sartoris (Faulkner) 31
Saudi Arabia 116
Scalia, Antonin 107
Scarlet Sister Mary (Peterkin) 30
Schirra, Walter 80
Schultz, George 102
Scopes, John *26*, 27
Securities Exchange Act (1934) 40
Sedition Act (1918) 19
segregation 66, 69, 72, 77
Selective Service Act (1948) 60
"separate but equal" doctrine 66, **67**
Seventeen (Tarkington) 17
Shame of the Cities, The (Steffens) 7
Sheik, The (Hull) 23
Shepard, Alan, Jr. 75
Sherman Anti-Trust Act 6
Silent Spring (Carson) 76
Simple Stakes a Claim (Hughes) 70
Simpson, Nicole Brown 115
Simpson, O. J. 115
Sinatra, Frank 117
Sinclair, Upton 8, 9, **10**, 24, 28
Sirhan, Sirhan 83
Sister Carrie (Dreiser) 5
Sixteenth Amendment 14
Skylab (space station) 90
Slaughterhouse-Five (Vonnegut) 85
Smith, Al 36
Smith, Alfred E. 30, 31
Smoot-Hawley Act (1930) 33

Snow White and the Seven Dwarves (film) 44
Soldiers' Pay (Faulkner) 27
Solzhenitsyn, Alexander 83
Sophie's Choice (Styron) 98
Souter, David 112
Southeast Asia Treaty Organization (SEATO) 68
Soviet Union 62, 72, 74, 85, 99, 111. *See also* communism
space exploration 75, 94, 116
space race 62
Spanish-American War 5
Spirit of the Border, The (Grey) 9
Spock, Benjamin 58
Sputnik 62, 70, 71
square deal 9
Stafford, Thomas 80
Stagecoach (film) 47
Stalin, Joseph 55, 56
Standard Oil Company 12, **15**
Star Trek (television show) 81
Star Wars (film) 86
Starr, Kenneth 117, 118
Stein, Gertrude 37
Steinbeck, John 44, 48, 51, 63
Steinem, Gloria **89**
Stevenson, Adlai 64
Stokes, Carl 83
Story of My Life, The (Keller) 6
Strategic Arms Limitation Treaty (SALT) 89
Strategic Arms Reduction Treaty (START II) 116
Straw Man, The (film) 14
Streets of Night (Dos Passos) 25
strikes 120*g*
    coal 7
    PATCO 101
subway system 5, 7
suffrage 24, 120*g*
Summerfield, Arthur 72
Sun Also Rises, The (Hemingway) 27
Supreme Court 17, 32
Susan Lenox: Her Fall and Rise (Phillips) 18
Susann, Jacqueline 81

T

Taft-Harley Act (1947) 59
Taft, William Howard 5
Tai-Pan (Clavell) 81
Tale of Two Cities, A (film) 41
Tar Baby (Morrison) 100
Tarzan of the Apes (Burroughs) 15

Teapot Dome trial 32
Teheran Conference 55
telephones **12**, 16, 76, 101–102
television 107
Tender is the Night (Fitzgerald) 39
Tennessee Valley Authority (TVA) 32, 38
test-tube baby 106
This Side of Paradise (Fitzgerald) 22
Thomas, Clarence 112
Thorpe, Jim 13, *13*
Three Lives (Stein) 10
Three Soldiers (Dos Passos) 23
Titanic (film) 117
Titanic sinking 13
To Kill a Mockingbird (Lee) 74
toga parties **97**
Tower Commission Report 107
Town Down by the River, The (Robinson) 11
toys **103**
Trail of the Lonesome Pines, The (Fox) 10
Tree Grows in Brooklyn, A (Smith) 53
trench warfare *19*
Triangle Shirtwaist Company fire 12
Truman, Harry S. 57–61, 63–64
trust-busting 6, 12, 101–102
Twain, Mark **8**
Twentieth Amendment 37
Twenty-fourth Amendment 76
Twenty-second Amendment 63
Twenty-seventh Amendment 88
Twenty-sixth Amendment **87**
Tydings-McDuffie Act (1934) 39
Typhoid Mary 9

U

UN Charter 57
unemployment 34, 35, 39, 42, 47, 92
unions 11, 15, 65, 101, 120*g*. *See also* strikes
United Nations 115
Up From Slavery (Washington) 6
Updike, John 83, 87, 100
Urey, Harold 33
Uris, Leon 95
U.S. Steel Corporation 6

V

Valley of the Dolls (Susann) 81
Versailles, Treaty of 11, 20

Vidal, Gore 78
Vietnam War 74, 79–84, 86–90, 94, 111
Viking space program 95
Villa, Pancho 17, *17*
Virginian, The (Wister) 6
Volstead Act (1920) 21, 22
Vonnegut, Kurt, Jr. 77, 85, 90
voting 113

W

Wallace, George 84
Walters, Barbara 95
War of the Worlds (Wells) 46
Warhol, Andy 77, 83
Warren Commission 78, 79
Warren, Robert Penn 106
Washington, Booker T. 6
Watergate Affair 89
Wells, H. G. 46
Wharton, Edith 8, 12, 22
Wilder, Thornton 45
Wilson, Woodrow 14–22
Wings of the Dove, The (James) 6
Wobblies, 8. *See also* Industrial Workers of the World
Wolfe, Tom 107
women 12, **16**, 37, **51**, **89**, 101
    abortion 90, 106
    birth control 15, 17
    rights movement 24. *See also* suffragists
Wonderful Wizard of Oz, The (Baum) 5
Woodstock Music and Art Fair 85
Works Progress Administration (WPA) 32, 41, 47
World According to Garp, The (Irving) 97
World Trade Center bombing *114*, 117
World War I 11, 14, 18–19, 21, 23
World War II 32–56, 62, 110
Wright, Orville 7
Wright, Wilbur 7

Y

Yalta Conference 56
Yeager, Charles "Chuck" 65
Yousef, Ramzi Ahmed 117
yuppie 99, 120*g*

Z

Zimmerman, Arthur 18